The Basic Book Of

Twining

The Basic Book Of

Twining

By Esther Warner Dendel

with Photographs and Drawings by Jo Dendel

VAN NOSTRAND REINHOLD COMPANY
New York   Cincinnati   Toronto   London   Melbourne

13.95

Designed by Loudan Enterprises

Published in 1978 by Van Nostrand Reinhold Company
A division of Litton Educational Publishing, Inc.
135 West 50th Street, New York, NY 10020, U.S.A.

Van Nostrand Reinhold Limited
1410 Birchmount Road
Scarborough, Ontario M1P 2E7, Canada

Van Nostrand Reinhold Australia Pty. Ltd.
17 Queen Street
Mitcham, Victoria 3132, Australia

Van Nostrand Reinhold Company Limited
Molly Millars Lane
Wokingham, Berkshire, England

Library of Congress Cataloging in Publication Data
Dendel, Esther Warner, 1910–
The basic book of twining.
Includes index.
1. Hand weaving. I. Title. II. Title: Twining.
TT848.D453   746.1'4   77-27428
ISBN 0-442-22078-2

Contents

Introduction

Everywhere in the world people use and love baskets. Many of man's needs—from gambling trays to coffins, from hats to sandals—have traditionally been met by baskets. The intense interest in basketry today is partly due to the ever-expanding variety of available material. Soft fibers, such as yarn, jute, raffia, and grasses, are being used as well as the more traditional rigid materials, such as cane and reeds. Using pliable materials enables more people to become adept at basketry. Even small children are able to master the skill.

In general, baskets can be divided into two categories—woven and coiled. Woven baskets, whether twined or plaited, are the ancestors of all loom weaving. Coiled basketry in its many variations leads to the needle and sewing. Basketry can be said to be the mother craft of all the fiber arts. The actual techniques of basketry have changed very little in hundreds of years. We are simply taking these techniques in more directions. That is the purpose of this book.

In this book I have focused on twining, a vast field in itself. The ease with which pattern can be introduced in coiled baskets has sometimes led to a neglect of form. My involvement in sculpture and in weaving has led to a personal bias toward twining, as opposed to coiling, although great baskets have been made by both methods. To me there is no basket more beautiful than one with the subtle curve, the simple shape, the understated decoration, and the beautiful craftsmanship of an old Pomo Indian basket, shown in Figure 4–1. Other artists will have other choices.

Twining is simply twisting. Being strictly a hand technique it takes us entirely away from machine civilization. For those of us who live in an over-industrialized society, this is part of its great appeal. Twining takes us far back into history. Sometime between 300 and 100 B.C., the people of ancient Peru twined the Parcus Band, which is one of the treasures of the Los Angeles County Museum. (Figure 1.) In North America blankets twined by the Chilkat Indians were marvels of pattern and workmanship. With cedar bark, sinew, and wool these ceremonial fabrics were made into articles of astonishing beauty. The one owned by the Brooklyn Museum measures 54 by 69 inches. It comes from southeastern Alaska. (Figure 2.)

Figure 1. The Parcas Band. An example of ancient Peruvian twining done in alpaca wool. Courtesy of Los Angeles County Museum of Art.

Figure 2. A ceremonial blanket twined by the Chilkat Indians of North America in wool, cedar bark, and sinew. Courtesy of the Brooklyn Museum.

Figure 3. A twined tote bag by Helen Hennessey.

Figure 4. A gentle breeze rocks Sean as he sleeps in his twined cradle by Fran Patten.

The historic family tree of twining is still flowering and growing, even though its roots are embedded in ancient cultures, which flourished long before Christ was born. Although recently made, Helen Hennessey's bag, made of glowing oranges and gold yarns with rich, earth browns, is a close relative of these older twinings. (Figure 3.) The cradle which Fran Patten twined for her baby is really a large basket twined with soft materials. (Figure 4.) By using soft fibers instead of stiff reeds belts, garments, and wall hangings come into being as easily as a basket. The wall hanging twined by Rosita Montgomery was inspired by a Japanese rain cape and drapes as softly as a garment. (Figure 5.)

Figure 5. A twined wall hanging by Rosita Montgomery, which was inspired by a Japanese rain cape.

In Ethiopia, twining is a lively art today. It is possible to buy a twined shepherd's hat right off a man's head while walking down a main street in Addis Ababa. The example shown here was purchased there in 1973. (Figure 6.) In the busy Addis market there are stalls piled high with twined rugs and mats, sometimes in color, but usually in natural tones of beige, black, and brown. Sturdy bags are made in all sizes and come in natural materials. (Figure 7.)

I visited the little village of Lalibela in a remote part of northern Ethiopia in the company of a group of craftsmen from America. Some of the members of our group were on their hands and knees examining the twined rug on the floor of the hotel dining room when one member said, "Look up." Above our heads was a bright fabric ceiling of red, blue, and beige—a great circle like a giant umbrella. It too was twined. (Figure 8.)

Figure 6. An Ethiopian shepherd's hat in natural, beige, brown, and black.

Figure 7. Twined rugs and mats in an Addis Ababa market.

Figure 8. A twined ceiling in the Seven Olives Hotel in Lalibela, Ethiopia. Photograph courtesy of Cindy Hickok.

The simplicity of the technique is one of the many charms of twining. With a few twigs pruned from a bush, a few lengths of yarn, and a few minutes of time an ordinary pot can be encircled by a distinctive plant holder. The one shown is by Barbara Kincaid. (Figure 9.) In its simplest form there are two classifications of cords, or elements, used in twining. Those which are *passive* have the others twisted around them. Almost everyone is familiar with the structure of twined baskets and can visualize the action. Two reed ends cross a third, which is at right angles to the two, enclosing it before again twisting over one another and crossing the next reed. (Figure 10.) Either the vertical or the horizontal strands may do the twisting, being the *active* element. Usually, the vertical cords are passive and are called the *warps*. The active pair, which twine around the warps, are called *wefts*. However, warps sometimes do the twining, as you'll see in chapter 13.

Figure 9. A twined pot holder by Barbara Kincaid.

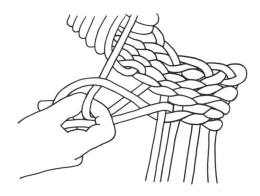

Figure 10. Twining with pliable warps.

10

CHAPTER 1.

Getting Started

THE TERMS: WARP AND WEFT

For beginning craftsmen, the terms *warp* and *weft* may be new. In weft twining there are two classifications of cords. The ones which are passive have the second set twisted around them. The passive ones are called *warps* and the ones that do the twisting are called *wefts*. Usually, two wefts encircle one warp, but there may be more than two wefts and they may encircle more than one warp. You will begin with the simplest kind of weft twining, which is two wefts encircling one warp. You may think of the warps as the "bones" beneath the surface of the completed twining.

Usually, the lower end of the warps hang free. It *is* possible to twine on fixed warps however, and this technique will be shown later in chapter 11. You will begin work here with the lower warp ends hanging free.

MATERIALS

Thick, heavy yarns, or cords, are most suitable for twining. Cotton rug yarn is quite generally available at yarn shops and from mail order catalogs. It makes an excellent warp, used either singly or with several strands together as one.

Mop cord is available in large spools from yarn shops that deal in special yarns for the craftsman working in the fabric arts. (See the list of suppliers in the back of the book.) Mop cord takes dye nicely, has a smooth, soft surface for the fingers to slide against, and is a good size for warp. It is my favorite warp for twining. Seine cord is also a satisfactory warp, although not as pliable as rug yarn or mop cord. It is generally available in shops handling macramé supplies.

Actually, any pliable material may be used for wefts. Heavy woolen rug yarn is especially desirable, because each twist is large enough to show as a unit.

EQUIPMENT

A variety of simple frames have been used in the past for twining. The American Indians stretched a cord between two stakes or trees and hung the warps from this cord.

The equipment I like best consists of a piece of building board and some T-pins. Wishing to keep the process as simple and as freely done as possible, this is all I ordinarily use. When making shaped articles (collars, clothing, etc.) I pin the work to the building board. When making cylindrical articles, such as pillows and bags, I cut a piece of building board the desired width and work around and around it. Covering the building board with fabric which has a pattern of woven squares is an aid in spacing the warps.

You will also need a pair of scissors to cut the yarns, a tape measure to check on the width at intervals, and a needle with a large eye and a blunt point to work in ends. A crochet hook and a roll of masking tape are sometimes useful. (Figure 1–1.)

Figure 1–1. Equipment needed to get started—building board covered with squared fabric, suitable fibers, curved needles, T-pins, crochet hook, and scissors.

Figure 1–2. Weft-twined pillow by the author. Twining was done around a 12-inch building board.

THE BEGINNING PROJECT: A TWINED PILLOW

For the learning project in simple weft twining I have selected a pillow. A bag can be made in the same way. Both the warp and the weft of this pillow are heavy woolen rug yarn—a three-ply twist. The finished size is 12 by 13 inches. It was made over a piece of building board, ½-inch-thick, cut a scant 12 inches wide. (Figure 1–2.)

The warps must be cut more than twice the desired length because each one is middled (doubled back over itself at midpoint). A few extra inches are needed at the ends for grasping as the work nears completion. For this project I cut my warps twice 1⅓ feet, or 2⅔ feet long. The number of warps needed varies with the material. With the yarn I used four warp ends (two pairs of yarns) were needed for each inch. Since it is 2 feet around the pillow, ninety-six ends (forty-eight pairs) were needed. To allow for the thickness of the edges (½ inch), the board was cut a scant 1 foot wide.

SECURING THE WARPS

The first step after cutting the warps is to secure them in place. There are three different ways to do this. In order to begin the actual twining as quickly as possible, you will begin the pillow with the simplest method. This consists of hanging each warp at the midpoint of its length on a cord which has been wrapped around the building board. Lark's head knots are used to fasten the warps to the cord. This method will be easy for those who have used the knot for starting macramé. For those who are not familiar with it, a simple drawing will suffice. (Figure 1–3.) Turn the knots over, so that the little horizontal bars will be on the back side. (Figure 1–4.)

This method does not space out the yarns the way they will be in the body of the twining. In order to know how many warps per inch will be needed with the particular material being used, it is necessary to make a small trial sample. If you're using the same materials I used, you already know that forty-eight pairs are needed altogether.

Alternate methods of securing the warps will be shown in chapter 12, where they will be a source of reference for other projects. On now to the pillow!

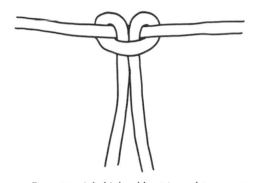

Figure 1–3. A lark's head knot is used to mount warps on a cord.

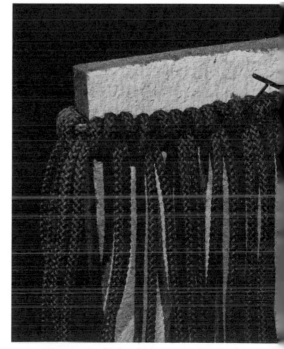

Figure 1–4. Lark's head knots turned to the back.

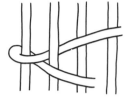

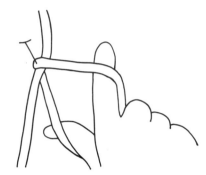

Figure 1–5. Wrapping warp with a middled weft.

Figure 1–6. Position one for the right hand.

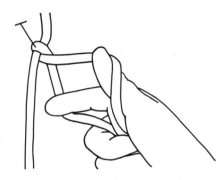

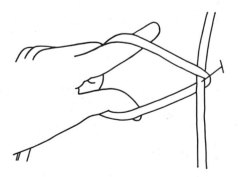

Figure 1–7. Position two for the right hand.

Figure 1–8. Position one for the left hand.

MAKING THE HAND MOTIONS

I selected a pillow for the learning piece because once the warps are in place, the work progresses around and around without change of direction or change of hand motion. It is important to get the "feel" of the simple flip of the wrist used in twining. Various craftsmen may alter the motion slightly, but it is basically the same all over the world. I will describe the action used for right-handed persons and then will show how to vary it for left-handed workers. With a little practice one can become ambidextrous by learning both ways.

Cut a length of weft yarn approximately 2 yards long. At midpoint of the length encircle any warp. (Figure 1–5.) Use a T-pin to secure in place.

Position one for the right hand: Insert thumb and index finger of the right hand between the wefts. The back of your hand is facing toward your body. (Figure 1–6.)

Position two for the right hand: Rotate hand downward toward your feet until your palm faces your body. Your hand has made a half-circle and the wefts are crossed. (Figure 1–7.)

Drop the wefts, pull a new warp (or pair of warps if two are being used as one) between the wefts, and resume the first position. Some craftsmen flip all of the warps up, above the line of twining, before they start and then bring them down, one at a time, as needed. Usually, the index finger of the hand which is not doing the swiveling is used to hook the warp through the wefts.

If the right hand rotates the wefts, the work progresses from left to right. In a tubular project like this one there is no need to reverse directions. However, in a flat piece, where the twining goes across the warps and then turns back, it is very useful to master the turn of the wrist with the left hand. The left-hand action is similar to the right but is illustrated here for clarity. (Figures 1–8 and 1–9.)

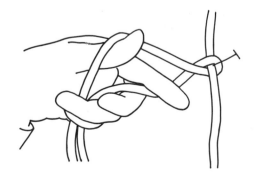

Figure 1–9. Position two for the left hand.

CONTROLLING THE TENSION

Tension is controlled simply by pulling on the warp ends, one at a time. It is much easier to pull down than to pull upward which is why you should twine from the top to the bottom of any piece you are doing. However, some experienced twiners prefer to start at the bottom and control tension by beating the wefts in place with a dog comb or other device.

STARTING NEW WEFTS

A new pair of wefts may be started at any place on the warps. Two wefts are temporarily knotted together and pinned down beside the place where they will actually begin to twine. The photograph shows the new weft started at the right of the twining, which is being done by the left hand. (Figure 1–10.) A right-handed worker will pin the new weft to the left of the area of work. The knot is later untied and each end is threaded through a needle and worked back into the twining on the wrong side.

The results of joining new wefts can be smoother if you arrange it so that only one is added at a time. This produces one used-up end and one new end at each joining of yarns. Both of these will be hidden later on the back side. If two wefts run out and two new ones are added at any one point in the work, you have the bother of dealing with four ends in one spot. Cutting the two wefts different lengths in the very beginning ensures that each will run out at a different place in the work; or, if a weft is doubled to begin with, fold it off-center.

The design in my pillow is of irregularly spaced stripes. When a new color was to be introduced, I started with a middled weft of the new color in order to avoid having four ends to dispose of in that spot. By doing this, there were only the two ends of the old wefts to deal with. The middled new weft was pinned in place until several twists had been made.

Figure 1–10. Starting a new pair of wefts. The knot will be untied later and the ends will be worked back into the twining on the wrong side.

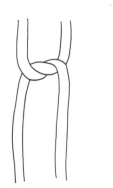

Figure 1–11. Square knot—step one.

Figure 1–12. Square knot—step two.

FINISHING THE PILLOW

When the twining had progressed as far as planned, I slipped the work off the building board, turned the pillow wrong side out, and tied the warp ends together. I tied a warp from the front to the opposite warp on the back of the lower layer, using square knots. (Figures 1–11 and 1–12.) I cut these warp ends about 1 inch from the knots, and they remain out of sight on the inside of the pillow. There are other ways to finish off a twining. You may, for example, "twine off" ends similarly to the way they are "twined on," as taught in chapter 12.

TWINING A BAG

If your twined cylinder is to be a bag instead of a pillow, you may want a decorative finish. In the edge of the bag shown, Helen Hennessey wrapped yarn around pairs of warps and secured the ends on the wrong side of the bag. The bag should be turned wrong side out to do this. A twined strap makes a good handle. (Figure 1–13.)

Figure 1–13. Wrapping warps at the bottom of a bag by Helen Hennessey.

CHAPTER 2.

More Basic Skills

By making the pillow shown in the last chapter, you learned one way to set warps in place and how to twine a cylinder. You need only a few further skills in order to undertake more projects. You need, for example, to learn how to turn around at either end of a flat piece of work and how to finish off the warp ends if it is not practical to tie them as was done with the pillow. You will also learn how to control the direction of the twist and how to make vertical and diagonal stripes. First, here is how to turn.

Figure 2–1. One method of turning around at the right edge. This method produces a small cross on the selvage.

TURNING AROUND

One way is to twine over the very last warp, twist the wefts again just as though there were another warp left, and then bend the wefts back in the direction from which they came. This method makes a small cross on the selvage which is sometimes desirable. At other times, you may wish for a smooth selvage. (Figure 2–1.)

A smooth edge or selvage is made by stopping the lower weft and turning it back one warp short of the end. The upper weft wraps the end warp twice before turning back. It is easy to see from the drawings that on the right-hand edge the weft which wraps the end warp passes *under* the warp next to the end as it reverses direction. Just the opposite is true at the left edge. (Figures 2–2 and 2–3.)

Note that neither one of these methods should be used if you are making vertical stripes.

Figure 2–2. Method of turning around at the right edge for a smooth selvage.

Figure 2–3. Method of turning around at the left edge for a smooth selvage.

MAKING COUNTERED TWINING

If you are twining a flat piece and using the same hand motions before and after turning around, the work will have a "knitted look." This is called *countered twining*. The photograph shows the texture of countered twining. (Figure 2–4.) In some projects, countered twining is very attractive. The pillow front by Louella Ballerino in countered rows uses stripes of rich color to accent the horizontal effect. (Figure 2–5.)

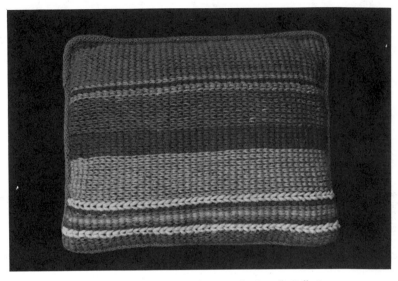

Figure 2–4. Appearance of countered twining.

Figure 2–5. A pillow top done in countered twining by Louella Ballerino.

AVOIDING COUNTERING

If you want to avoid countered rows, you have a choice of methods. You may simply turn the work over at the end of each row so that the "wrong," or underside, comes topmost. This enables you to again work from left to right, which usually is easier for right-handed persons. After the second row, turn the work back to the original position. The side of the work facing up alternates with each row.

For bag handles and other narrow projects, flopping the work at the end of each row is no trouble. However, it becomes a nuisance on larger pieces and on work which is pinned to a pattern, so you might as well learn the left-hand motions shown in Figures 1–8 and 1–9. At first, they may seem awkward, but after a few rows, you'll get the feel of them. Another alternative is to continue using the right hand for the twisting motion, but making the twist toward the body, instead of away from it on alternate rows.

Managing the direction of slant of the twisted wefts becomes more easily understandable if you think about the letters S and Z. The central portion of the letter Z slants one way (/) and the central portion of the letter S slants another (\). One has only to look at the work to know whether an S twist or a Z twist has been produced. A Z twist is produced when the wrist is rotated away from the body in left-to-right work. An S twist is produced when the wrist is rotated toward the body in left-to-right work.

When Jo Dendel twined his large rug (Figure 9–6) he placed the warps in a clamp which he hung on a frame he could walk around. This enabled him to use the same hand motions throughout. He did not want countered twining because the twining does not pack together as solidly as it does when the wefts all slant in the same direction.

MAKING VERTICAL STRIPES

If two wefts of different colors are used and if each twist of weft is a simple crossing made with a half-turn of the wrist, each color will come to the surface over alternate warps. In order to "come out even"—light–dark, light–dark, etc.—an even number of warps is needed.

One word of caution: For vertical stripes you should not use the methods described in this chapter to turn around. Those methods will bring light under dark or dark under light and destroy the stripe pattern. Instead, you must twine over the very last warp, making a twist after crossing it. Bend the weft which crossed on the top surface back in the direction from which it came. It simply turns around on the top surface, but is held in place by the lower weft, which turns around also, but behind the last warp. If the lighter weft shows, pull it a little tighter until it disappears from sight. (Figure 2–6.) The effectiveness of a band of vertical stripes is shown in this beautiful basket from Ghana. (Figure 2–7.)

Vertical stripes take on a zigzag edge when done in countered twining. This bag from Ethiopia was twined as a flat piece which was later sewn together at the sides. (Figure 2–8.)

Figure 2–6. Method of turning around to keep light under light and dark under dark on the return row.

Figure 2–7. A bag from Ghana showing vertical stripes.

Figure 2–8. The zigzag effect of vertical stripes in countered twining is shown in this bag from Ethiopia. From the collection of Mr. and Mrs. Jo Dendel.

Figure 2–9. A Nez Perce bag twined with corn husks, string, and wool.

MAKING HORIZONTAL STRIPES

The Nez Perce Indians made masterful bags of corn husks twined with grocery store string. According to legend, the husks were made silky and soft by chewing. This was women's work and laborious, so it became important to use the husks on the top surface where they would show. Any other sturdy fiber would do for the inside of the bags, which would be lined with calico. By using one weft of husk and one of string, and by making two half-turns, or a complete rotation, the husks could be kept always on the top surface of the bag. Woolen yarn, which was scarce, was used for the colored design areas. In the earlier Nez Perce bags, a native hemp was twisted into string. (Figure 2–9.) You can follow the technique of the Nez Perce Indians to twine horizontal bands, or stripes, of one color or fiber.

A study of a fiber bag from Ethiopia shows some of the possibilities. Note the solid horizontal rows contrasted with bands of stripes. An added feature of this bag is that the warps for the handle are continuous, from the bottom of one side to the bottom of the other side. The body of the bag was twined around and around; the handle above the opening was twined from side to side. The handle truly is an integral part of the bag. (Figure 2–10.)

Figure 2–10 A fiber bag from Ethiopia. The solid horizontal bands contrast with the vertical stripes.

MAKING DIAGONAL STRIPES

When twining with two wefts—one light and one dark—turn back at the edge as explained earlier in this chapter under "How to Turn Around." This will produce a pattern of dark under light, light under dark, etc. across the row. Several rows continued in this way will produce diagonal stripes. Several rows of S twist followed by several rows of Z twist will produce a chevron design. (Figure 2–11.)

As soon as one knows how to make vertical stripes, horizontal stripes, and diagonal stripes in either direction, all sorts of designs can be made with these components. A hat twined by Ann Daniels shows some of the simple designs possible by making full and half-twists with wefts of two colors. (Figure 2–12.) Joan Onaga's sampler shows other possible motifs. (Figure 2–13.) One red weft and one white weft were used and the desired color was brought to the surface by using either a half-twist or two half-twists.

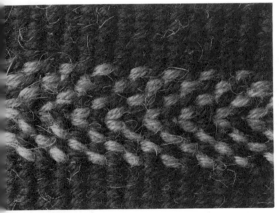

Figure 2–11. Chevron design. Four rows of Z twist followed by four rows of S twist.

Figure 2–12. A twined hat by Ann Daniels.

Figure 2-13. A sampler by Joan Onaga showing the design variations possible by varying half-twists with two half-twists, thus controlling the surface color.

ENDING SMOOTHLY

There are several ways to end a twining, just as there are several ways to begin. The simplest way is to thread the warp ends, one at a time, through a needle, and work them back into the twining. Each warp is threaded through a needle in turn and worked back under the weft that covers the adjacent warp. (Figure 2-14.) The warp at the end will have no obvious place to go, so turn the work over and bring the remaining warp under the wefts at the back in the row next to it. Then snip the warp ends close to the twining.

Another method of ending, which is called "twining off," is shown in chapter 12.

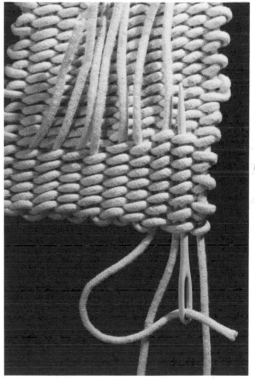

Figure 2-14. Ending a twining by working the warp ends back under the wefts.

CHAPTER 3.

Shaping

There are several ways to shape a twined article. The ancient Peruvians made twined sandals which were shaped to fit their feet; the Chilkat Indians shaped their blankets to fit their shoulders; Ethiopian twiners shape hats to fit their heads; and baskets are twined in an almost endless array of shapes. Rows of warp may be added or decreased, partial rows of weft may be used to widen an area, and tension may be varied, compacting the wefts in some areas. All of these methods are simple in technique.

Necklaces and collars made by twining are good pieces on which to practice shaping. I will describe here how to make a yarn necklace and three different collars, each of which solve shaping problems by the addition of either wefts or warps.

YARN NECKLACE WITH SHAPED NECK AREA

Cotton rug yarn for warp and an assortment of thinner yarns in blues, greens, grays, and black for weft were selected by Louella Ballerino for the necklace. She used two rug yarns together as one cord for each warp to produce a ridgy texture. (Figure 3–1.)

Twenty warps were cut, each 4⅓ feet long. Twining began at the center of the length of the warps (which is the back-of-the-neck portion of the necklace) instead of at one end. This eliminated the need to pull the entire length of each warp through the twisted wefts. It is a technique that speeds up the work, especially on large projects where unusually long warps are required.

To begin work at midpoint of the warp lengths group them into pairs, tie them together at their midpoints in overhand knots (Figure 3–2), and then pin them beside one another on a piece of building board. Middle a length of weft, enclose the first warp with it, and twine across all the warps. The temporary overhand knots may be untied at any time after the twining is underway. (Figure 3–3.) But before you progress too far, read on about shaping.

Figure 3–1. A yarn necklace by Louella Ballerino.

The area encircling the back of the neck in this particular necklace needs to be shaped. The front of the necklace does not have to be shaped, since it was not designed to follow the neckline in the way that a collar does.

SHAPING BY CHANGING TENSION

The simplest way to shape a twined article is to pull on some of the warps, one at a time, thus compacting the wefts which have been twined. The tension may be tightened a bit or considerably, depending on need. Figure 3–4 shows a sample of twining as it appears before the warps have been pulled and Figure 3–5 shows the same sample after the tension has been adjusted. In the curved piece, the warp nearest the left edge was pulled most. Each successive warp was pulled a bit less. This can be gauged by the eye.

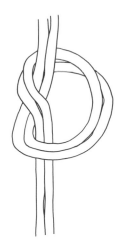

Figure 3–2. Overhand knot.

Figure 3–3. Starting to twine at the center of the length of the warps.

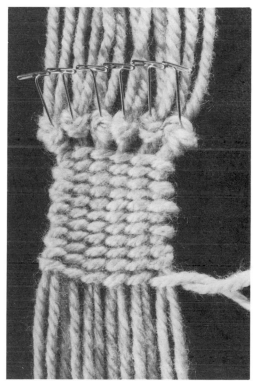

Figure 3–4. Twining sample with even tension.

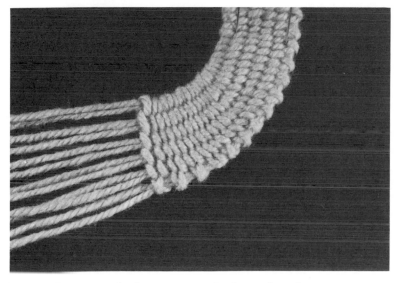

Figure 3–5. Twining sample after warp tension has been tightened.

25

SHAPING BY ADDING PARTIAL ROWS

In the yarn necklace and in the collars which follow some shaping was accomplished by adding partial rows of weft. Add a *single* partial row by dropping a middled weft over any *interior* warp and twining to the outside edge. In the drawing it is shown as a dark row. (Figure 3–6.) Add two partial rows by starting with a middled weft around the *outside* warp. Twine in toward the center. When several warps have been encompassed, turn back just as though you had reached the end of the warps. (Figure 3–7.) When you have twined back to the edge where the added rows were started, turn around and twine back across *all* the warps. (Figure 3–8.) In the illustration the added rows are shown in a light value to distinguish them clearly. In actual work, however, if the additions are done in the same color as the area to which they are being added, they will barely show. Pull on the warps to tighten the work and compact the twining. The collar will begin to assume a circular shape as soon as even two partial rows have been added.

The number of partial rows which need to be added depends upon the materials used and whether the curve to be achieved is a gradual, slow curve or a quickly curving area. You will judge the need as you go along and act accordingly. Generally, though, adding more than two partial rows at one time will result in an undesirable bulge.

Both of the shaping methods described above—shaping by changing tension and shaping by adding partial rows—were incorporated into Louella's necklace for the slight shaping at the back of the neck.

FINISHING THE NECKLACE

When Louella cut a length of weft for the first part of the necklace, she cut off an exact length to use later for the second part of the necklace. This was a convenient way to make certain that the two sides of the necklace matched.

After twining for 1⅓ feet, Louella went back to the middle of the length of warps, the place she had begun work, and started twining toward the opposite end for 1⅓ feet. Now and then, she placed the two ends of the band side by side to be sure the blocks of solid color and stripes were matching. When the second half had been twined for 1⅓ feet, she brought the two ends together and twined across *all* of the warps, uniting the two bands.

The untwined warps ends form the fringe. To give extra fullness to the fringe, Louella tied in some additional dark yarns in front of the cotton warps.

Figure 3–6. Adding a single partial row of weft.

Figure 3–7. Adding two partial rows of weft—step one.

Figure 3–8. Adding two partial rows of weft—step two.

COLLAR I

By measuring around the *outer* edge of a collar pattern, I found that to make a twined collar 5 inches wide, the outside warps need to be 3½ feet long. Adding 6 inches for ease of handling at the finish gave me a measurement of 4 feet. Since the warps are middled in the "twining-on" process, the outside ones had to be cut twice 4 feet, or 8 feet long. There are sixteen warp ends in the collar (eight lengths before they were middled during the "twining-on"). Their lengths varied progressively from the shorter 3¾-feet ones in the interior to the longest, 8-feet ones at the outside. When in doubt about how long to cut the in-between warps, I tried to err on the side of wastage rather than shortage.

The first step after the warps had been cut and arranged in order of their progressive lengths was to twine them into place. The warp material is a greenish black rug yarn. The weft yarns are red, orange, yellow, maroon, and pink. Many of the partial rows added for shaping are in the greenish black color. (Figure 3–9.)

If you work over a paper pattern pinned to a board, it is easy to see where partial rows of weft need to be added to make the collar conform to the pattern. If you are holding the work in your fingers and not working over a pattern, frequent references to a mirror are helpful. In order to have some handwork while flying to Africa in 1972, I started the collar shown without any pattern and without pinning it to anything. Using only my fingers, I held the work in my lap. This gave me the satisfaction of knowing that a shaped article may be twined without using any equipment at all.

Figure 3–9. A collar twined by the author without pinning.

FINISHING THE COLLAR

When the collar was completed, I disposed of the warps by working them back into the twining on the wrong side. I threaded each one in turn into a needle with a blunt point. Beginning at the bottom edge, I took the lowest warp back in the direction from which it came, threading it into the "tunnel" between the twining in the second row from the bottom edge. I worked the second warp from the bottom edge back into the fourth row, etc. By skipping a row, instead of using an adjacent row, the finish appeared more like the beginning where the "twining on" began the collar. (See chapters 1 and 12 for descriptions of "twining on".)

I used the last two warps at the top of the collar on the right-hand end to make a fastening. Buttonhole stitching, with one of the warps over a loop in another, was used for this loop fastener. On the other side of the collar a knot which formed a yarn button was fastened into the warp.

COLLAR II

Louella Ballerino's collar is circular and large enough to slip over the head. (Figure 3–10.) The shaping devices are the same as those already described. Instead of beginning at one end of the warps and twining to the other, Louella began work in the center of the warp lengths. When both halves of the collar had been twined, there was a set of warps to dispose of at each end.

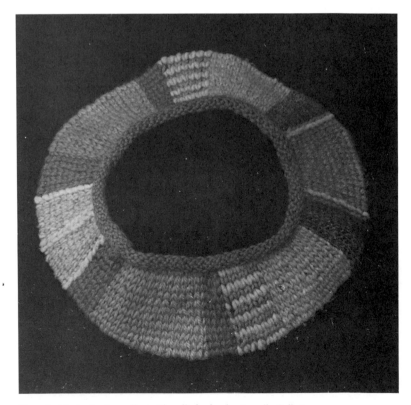

Figure 3–10. A circular collar with rolled edge by Louella Ballerino.

To be sure the collar was solidly joined at the center back and would never pull loose, Louella tied a warp fom one side to the corresponding warp from the other side in every third row, using a square knot. These knots are hidden by the twining, which she spread out to cover them. She then threaded the ends into a needle and worked underneath the twining on the wrong side. She worked the untied ends at the center back underneath the twining, too, but worked forward in the direction they were already going, instead of turning back in the direction from which they came.

Louella worked out an attractive rolled braid for the inside edge of her collar. This was her own invention so I have named it after her. You will find it described below as the "Ballerino Rolled Edge."

In the necklace and collars described so far, they were shaped by adding partial rows of *wefts*. I will also give directions for shaping by adding *warps*.

THE BALLERINO ROLL

The Ballerino roll is a rolled edging which has countless uses. It can be made with any number of yarns, depending on the width desired and the thickness of the yarn or cords. It is basically a simple half hitch worked back and forth across the warps. The take-up is considerable, but it varies with every size of warp, so it is desirable to make a test sample to determine how long to cut the warps. Secure them under the clip of a clipboard or tie them into a loop of yarn.

Step one: Pick up the first cord on the right side with the right hand. Hold the second warp taut with the left hand. Make a half hitch with yarn 1 around yarn 2 and pull it snug, as shown in the drawing. (Figure 3–11.)

Step two: Pick up the second warp in the right hand and hold the third warp taut with the left hand. Make a half hitch with warp 2 around warp 3 as shown in the drawing. (Figure 3–12.) Continue in this manner across all the warps. There will not be a warp for the end warp to wrap around so it simply hangs.

Step three: Reverse directions by picking up the first warp at the left in the left hand. Hold the warp next to it taut with the right hand. Half hitch warp 1 around warp 2. Continue in this manner across all the warps. (Figure 3–13.)

When the roll is sewn to a collar, the edge of a bag, or any surface where an edging is needed only one edge needs to be attached, as the roll will curl tightly around on itself. The photograph shows the appearance of the roll after it has progressed for a few rows. (Figure 3–14.)

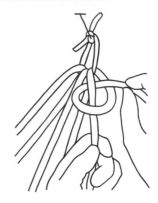

Figure 3–11. The Ballerino Roll—step one.

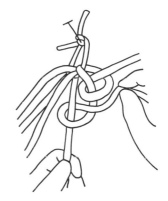

Figure 3–12. The Ballerino Roll—step two.

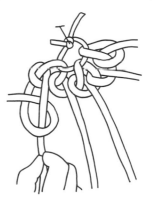

Figure 3–13. The Ballerino Roll—step three.

Figure 3–14. Appearance of the Ballerino Roll after a few rows.

COLLAR III

In the two collars already shown, the warps run the long direction and the weft twining goes across the narrow dimension, from the neck to the outside edge of the collar (and back again). Jean Hudson twined a collar which is exactly opposite in concept. In Jean's collar, the *warps* run from the neck to the outside edge and shaping is done by adding warps. (Figures 3–15 and 3–16.) The design inspiration for Jean's collar was a Masai beaded collar from Tanzania. (Figure 3–17.)

When rattail cord is braided, the changes of color in each loop catch the light somewhat in the manner of beads. To take advantage of this quality, Jean braided some of the warps in four-strand, round braids. The other warps are unbraided rattail cord. Some chenille yarn and thick-to-thin yarns were added to give additional textures. The colors are magenta, orange, purple, gold, red, and hot pink.

Figure 3–15. A collar shaped by the addition of warps by Jean Hudson.

Figure 3–16. Detail of collar in Figure 3–15.

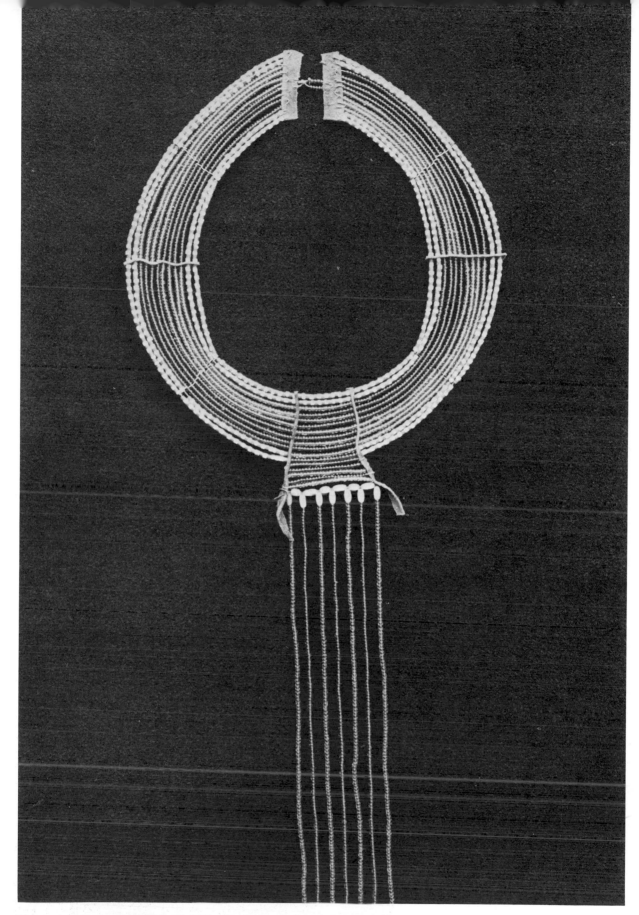

Figure 3-17. This Masai beaded collar from Tanzania was the inspiration for the collar in Figure 3-15.

To begin, ten braids, each 2 feet long, and two braids, each 3 yards long, were braided. These were middled in the "twining on" process, and were treated like ordinary, plain strands. Four extra-long braids were placed in the center front, giving eight long ends in that area.

Three plain, unbraided ends of rattail were used for warp between each braided warp. Fifty of these plain warps were cut, each 1 foot long, yielding 100 ends, each about 6 inches long.

After the beginning row of twining, which secured all of these warps, Jean pinned the work over a commerical collar pattern. No new warps were added until the seventh row of twining. Twenty-three unbraided lengths of rattail warps were added in this row, giving a spacing of seven plain warps between each braided warp. (Figure 3–18.) (I will describe how to add warps as soon as I have completed the count of added warps in this particular collar.) With different material, this count would not be correct, and should serve only as a guide. You would add whatever number is necessary to follow the paper pattern.

In Jean's collar it was necessary to again add warps in the seventeenth row. Three more long, braided warps were added at the center front and twenty 8-inch-long plain warps were added at intervals around the collar. This gave seven plain warps between the braided warps. (Figure 3–19.) Thirty rows of twining completed the collar. In other materials the number of rows, as well as the number of warps, would vary. A button made of a knot in the rattail cord on one side of center back and a loop on the other side made the fastening arrangement. The long braided warps were weighted with beads. (Figure 3–20.)

Figure 3–18. Detail of the collar showing seven plain warps between braided warps.

Figure 3–19. Detail of the collar showing braided strands used for some of the warps.

Figure 3–20. The back view of the collar.

32

SHAPING BY ADDING WARPS

Ordinarily, extra warps are added by pinning a middled warp in the space where extra width is needed. (Figure 3–21.) As the twining reaches the added warp, both the existing warp next to the added one and the first end of the added one are encircled as though they were one warp. (Figure 3–22.) The next twist encloses the other half of the added warp and the existing warp next to it, again, as though they were one. (Figure 3–23.)

The twining continues. On the next row the first end of the added warp is still treated as one of a pair with the old warp. (Figure 3–24.) The second end, however, is separated from the old warp and twined as a new cord. This gives a more gradual addition than if *both* new ends were twined over on the second row. (Figure 3–25.) On the third row both new ends are utilized separately and twined over.

The back of Jean's collar is fastened by a button made out of rattail and a loop.

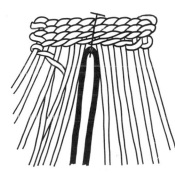

Figure 3–21. Pinning an added middled warp in place.

Figure 3–22. Enclosing the first half of the new middled warp.

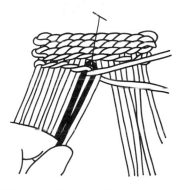

Figure 3–23. Enclosing the second end of the added warp.

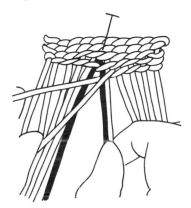

Figure 3–24. Treating the old and new ends as a single warp on the first half of the second row.

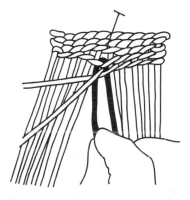

Figure 3–25. Separating one new end from the old warp.

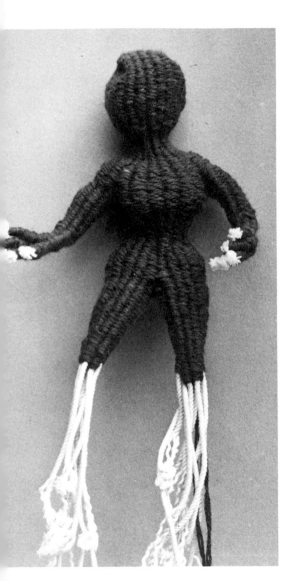

Figure 3-26. "Melissa" in process by Doris Fox.

Figure 3-27. The finished doll—"Melissa" by Doris Fox. The shaping was accomplished by separating and grouping warps to expand and contract to the contours of the figure.

SHAPING OVER CARDBOARD

Simple shapes may be cut from cardboard, which is used as a gauge to suggest when warps need to be added or dropped. See chapter 7 for more information.

SHAPING BY EYE

It is great fun to attempt to shape a figure entirely by eye. To get started on "Melissa," Doris Fox twined a square in the middle of the length of each of two sets of six warps. These squares were laid across each other at right angles. The next row of twining used all of the warps projecting from both squares, bringing them into a circular shape. This is a common way to begin twining baskets. The neck was narrowed by using two warps as one. By using each warp separately and by adding warps the shoulders were formed. (Figure 3-26.) The finished doll has convincing proportions, and making it was a real learning experience. (Figure 3-27.)

By using the simple ways of shaping described here, almost any shape can be achieved.

34

CHAPTER 4.

Baskets

Perhaps there is no better way to begin the exciting study of baskets than to analyze great baskets of the past. Many collectors feel that the baskets made by the Pomo Indians of northern California are among the finest. The Pomo are of great interest to me because of the many techniques they combined, often in one basket, which are applicable to other textile projects.

I will start with an old Pomo basket, examining the way it was begun, the techniques used to develop it, the way it was decorated, and the way it was finished. You will then have acquired the knowledge to enable you to make many and varied baskets, applying each skill in your own way. (Figure 4–1.)

Figure 4–1. A Pomo Indian basket.

The materials will be different from the willow withes, sedge roots, bulrush roots, and redbud twigs gathered by the Pomo Indian women. These women went to a great deal of trouble to collect the materials they needed. They knew just what time of year to harvest each one. It would add another dimension to the current enthusiasm for basketry if each of you explored your own environment for suitable vegetation. In almost every part of the country there are suitable natural growths. However, we can begin very nicely with jute for the spokes, or warps, and raffia for the wefts. By using these tractable materials we can get into the process sooner.

The Pomo basket shown begins with two sets of eight warps crossed at right angles to each other at the bottom. A length of weft wraps them tightly together. (Figure 4–2.)

Instead of beginning twining immediately, 1 inch of three-strand braiding on the warps was next carried out. This is characteristic of Pomo baskets. When the braiding is pushed tightly together, it does not look like a braiding, however, because one sees only the edge of the strands. This method makes a sturdy center. The photographs showing the steps of braiding on warps have the braiding strands arranged loosely so the eye can follow each one. In actual practice, however, they are pulled snug and packed tightly.

Figure 4–2. The bottom of the Pomo basket showing eight warps crossed at right angles to each other.

Figure 4–3. Three-strand braiding on warps—part one, motion one.

Figure 4–5. Three-strand braiding on warps—part one, motion three.

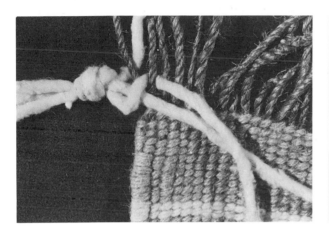

Figure 4–4. Three-strand braiding on warps—part one, motion two.

Figure 4–6. Three-strand braiding on warps—part two, motion one.

THREE-STRAND BRAIDING ON WARPS

Part one: Secure the three strands to be braided with an overhand knot. Later you will untie the ends and work them under the wefts with a needle. Think of the warps as 1, 2, 3, etc. Think of the three braiding strands as A, B, and C. If you encounter any difficulty in keeping track, tie small identifying tags on the braiding strands. Pick up braiding strand A (the first one), place it under warp 1, and lead it to the *right*. (Figure 4–3.) Pick up braiding strand B and place it under warp 2 as shown, and lead it to the *left*. (Figure 4–4.) Pick up braiding strand C, place it under warp 3 as shown, and lead it to the *right*. (Figure 4–5.) For part one, think "right, left, right."

Part two: You have used each of the braiding strands once. You will now use each of them again, but this time your thinking will be, "left, right, left." Pick up braiding strand A. (Here is where little tags come in handy during the learning process.) Lead strand A under warp 4 and lead it to the left. (Figure 4–6.) Pick up braiding strand B and bring it under warp 5. Lead it to the *right*. (Figure 4–7.) Pick up braiding strand C, bring it under warp 6, and lead it to the *left*. (Figure 4–8.)

Simply repeat these steps for the distance that is to be braided. Braiding gives a more durable bottom to the basket than simple twining, and this is probably the reason the Pomo made much use of it. They always braided on the outside surface of the basket; each braiding strand crosses two warps on the outside of the basket and only one on the inside.

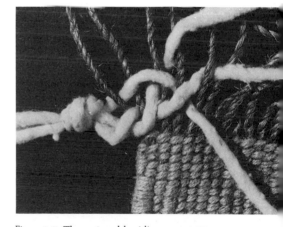

Figure 4–7. Three-strand braiding on warps —part two, motion two.

Figure 4–8. Three-strand braiding on warps—part two, motion three.

ADDING NEW SPOKES

Even before the three-strand braided area is completed, new spokes, or warps, must be added as the size increases. In the Pomo basket single spokes of willow are sharpened and inserted in the braided area. In your own basket, which will be made of softer material, you will add the new warps in pairs as described in chapter 3. The Pomo basket has ninety-six warps in use just 1½ inch from the beginning. You will remember that there were sixteen to start with at the center—an increase of six times the beginning.

The number of warps that you add determines the shape of the basket. You must also consider the number of warps required to execute a pattern, if a definite geometric design is to be used. For instance, twenty-two warps are needed for one unit of the geometric design on one small basket in my collection. The design is repeated ten times around the top of the basket, thus requiring 220 warps. The craftswoman who made it encountered a problem, because she had not added quite enough warps, and two of the design units are short by four warps. Instead of seeming like a defect, however, this imperfection further endears the basket to me. (Figure 4–9.)

Figure 4–9. A basket whose design unit requires twenty-two warps for each motif.

Figure 4-10. Three-strand twining—step one.

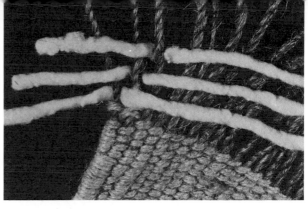

Figure 4-12. Three-strand twining—step three.

Figure 4-11. Three-strand twining—step two.

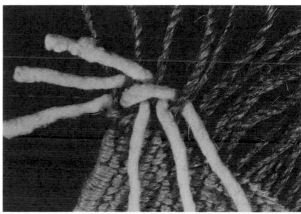

Figure 4-13. Three-strand twining—step four.

THREE-STRAND TWINING

If you were to simply look at the bottom of the Pomo basket you would not be able to tell whether the first rows of twining were a three-strand braiding or a three-strand twining. When several rows are compacted these two techniques look alike, although the technique is different. I have called the beginning work "three-strand braiding on warps." According to the great authority, Otis Tufton Mason, all Pomo twined baskets start that way. Mr. Mason gives many more interesting facts in his book, *Aboriginal Indian Basketry*. This lovely book was originally published by the Smithsonian Institution in 1902, but has been reissued by the Rio Grande Press, Inc. of Glorieta, New Mexico.

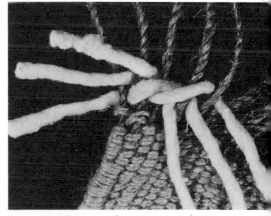

Figure 4-14. Three-strand twining—step five.

Actually, three-strand twining is simpler than three-strand braiding on warps and is an excellent technique to master. It is often used as a finish at the top of baskets around the rim. I present it here for comparison with three-strand braiding. Follow the photographs for instructions. (Figures 4-10 through 4-15.)

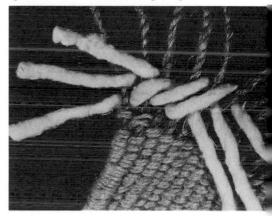

Figure 4-15. Three-strand twining—step six.

LATTICE TWINING

Following the braided area on the bottom of the Pomo basket is another reinforced area. It is done by a technique for which the Pomo are famous and is called "tee" in the Pomo language, meaning "lattice twining" in English. One weft lies along the top surface of the warps at right angles to them. Two other wefts are twined around the warps *and the passive weft*. (Figures 4–16 and 4–17.)

Lattice twining was used by the Pomo to make strong sieves and strainers. In the beautiful example shown here notice the reinforced bottom. (Figures 4–18 and 4–19.)

Figure 4–16. Lattice twining—step one.

Figure 4–17. Lattice twining—step two.

Figure 4–18. This Pomo strainer is an example of lattice twining. From the collection of Mr. and Mrs. Oakley Parker.

Figure 4–19. The bottom of the Pomo strainer.

TWINING THE CENTER SECTION

There are many ways to start a basket other than the crossed warps of the Pomo basket. One way is a method that provides a double layer of twining on the bottom of the basket—a good reinforcing device. Two sets of warps are cut. Each set is twined in its center section until the twined distance is equal to the width, or, in other words, until the twined section is a square. (Figure 4–20.) These squares are then placed one on top of the other, with the warps in one square projecting at right angles to those in the other. They are joined by twining a row around all the warps. (Figure 4–21.)

Figure 4–20. Beginning a basket by twining two squares in the middle of the length of the warps.

Figure 4–21. The two squares are placed at right angles, one on top of the other, and twined together.

When the Ethiopians weave their beautiful boat-shaped winnowing trays, they use a technique similar to this. They start twining in the center of the length of the warps and twine to either end, dropping warps to narrow the width as they go along. The warps, or spokes, which run the long way are round reeds. The twining material often in use in Ethiopia and northern Kenya is the casing of small roots. (Figure 4–22.)

Figure 4–22. A boat-shaped basket from Ethiopia. From the collection of Helen Wood Pope.

Figure 4-23. Plain weaving to begin a basket by Helen Hennessey.

Figure 4-24. The back of the basket in Figure 4-23 showing finish.

WEAVING THE CENTER

A small amount of plain weaving (instead of twining) is sometimes done in the center area of warps. This is the method used by Helen Hennessey to make her twined tray. The material she used was sisal. When she reached the rim of the tray, upon which it was to sit, she bent back the twining at the edge and made a double layer back toward the center section. (Figures 4–23 and 4–24.)

Still another method of weaving the center is to begin by weaving groups of warps for a short distance. For example, sixteen warps in groups of four may be interwoven, divided into twos, and then woven around. (Figures 4–25 and 4–26.)

A variation of this is to begin with eight warps, grouped in twos and then woven. (Figure 4–27.)

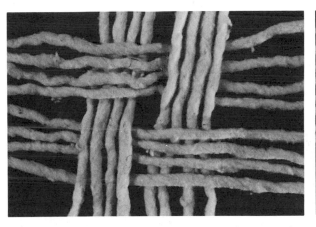

Figure 4–25. Beginning a basket. Sixteen warps are interwoven in groups of fours.

Figure 4–26. Beginning a basket. Groups of four warps are divided into twos.

Figure 4–27. Another way of beginning a basket. Eight warps are interwoven in pairs.

Figure 4–28. In this basket by Cindy Wallace, raffia weft is twined around jute warps.

FINISHING A BASKET

The Pomo basket is finished with three-strand braiding on the warps, after which they are simply cut off. There are many other ways to finish, however, and when you are using pliable material it is not satisfactory to cut the spokes close to the wefts. One of the best finishes is called "twining off" and is shown in detail in chapter 12. Another way is to bend the warp ends at right angles to the work and wrap over them with the weft material. Several baskets illustrated in this chapter are finished in this manner. Notice especially the basket in Figure 4–28.

MATERIALS FOR BASKETS

In my experience I have made considerable use of the ornamental flax plant whose strap-like leaves yield long fibers. Jute and raffia are the materials often used by Cindy Wallace for her baskets. The warps are jute and the twining is done with raffia. Her baskets are simple in shape and sturdy. (Figure 4–28.) Sisal is the material most often used by Helen Hennessey, although she sometimes introduces her own handspun yarn in the wefts. Her group of baskets show interesting variations of material and shape. (Figure 4–29.)

Figure 4–29. A group of baskets by Helen Hennessey made of handspun yarns, sisal, and unspun sisal.

Figure 4–30. Basket made by Helen Hennessey from sisal that was unraveled from a rug.

Several baskets have been made with the leftover squares of a sisal rug. (Figure 4–30.)

We tend to think of baskets as sturdy and enduring and many of them are. But there is also a place for the temporary, often playfully made, fragile basket, which may be used once or twice or not at all. When Helen Hennessey pruned her ivy, it occurred to her that instead of discarding the trimmings she might twine them into a quickly made little basket for limited use. (Figure 4–31.)

Figure 4–31. A temporary basket made of twigs by Helen Hennessey.

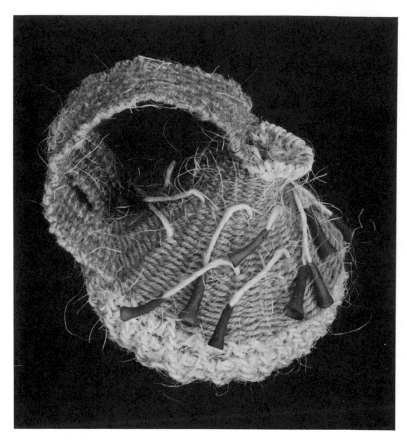

Figure 4–32. Sisal basket with eucalyptus seeds by Helen Hennessey.

ADDING DECORATION

In many contemporary baskets the addition of decoration seems to merely disguise what often is poor form. A beautiful shape is the first requisite of a beautiful basket. A basket to hold dried weeds was twined in sisal by Helen Hennessey and much thought was given in planning its beautiful shape. Notice that the eucalyptus seeds used as decoration do not detract from the form. (Figure 4–32.)

CHAPTER 5.

A Special Project: A Boxed Bag

This project is a sturdy bag with boxed sides. The handle is an integral part of the bag, having been twined in, from the bottom upwards. The only equipment required is an empty box which is light in weight and can be carried about. It will be used as a form. A flap covers the top opening. I used three-strand jute for the warp, except for the sides. The warp on the sides and the weft are rug yarn.

The box I used came with typing paper and measures approximately 8¾ by 11 inches. It is 2½ inches deep, which gives that dimension to the sides of the bag. Using two lengths of jute for each single warp, I cut sixty-four lengths to give thirty-two warps. To determine their length I measured all around the box lengthwise (11 + 2½ + 11 + 2½), which came to 27 inches. Adding 8 inches for the flap and 4 inches at either end for grasping (another 8 inches), a length of 43 inches for the warps was established.

I began twining across the warps in the central area, but not in the exact center of the length. I started the first row of twining 8 inches short of the center, because this area of twining makes the bottom of the bag and I had allowed for an 8-inch flap on one side. A temporary row of overhand knots above the first row of twining kept the warps from slipping. (Figure 5–1.) When the bottom of the bag was twined, I added warps at the ends to form the sides. These needed to be longer than the other warps because they were used to make the handle. I cut them twice 2½ feet or 5 feet long and attached them to the bottom of the bag at midpoint of their length. Two strands were used as one. Ten pairs were required on each side. (Figure 5–2.)

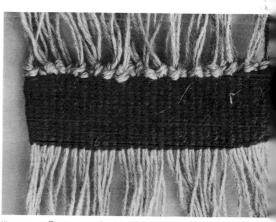

Figure 5–1. Beginning the bag by twining the bottom. The overhand knots are temporary.

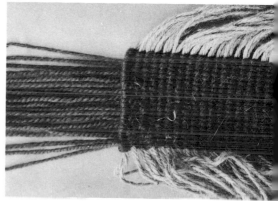

Figure 5–2. Adding warps at the ends, which will form the sides and the handle.

49

Figure 5–3. Twining around the box. The chevron design is made by four rows of Z twist followed by four rows of S twist.

Figure 5–4. The finished bag. The ends of the warps on the sides were tied together and wrapped to make the handle.

As soon as the side warps were added, the twining progressed around and around the box. When the work was 2 inches from the bottom, I introduced a chevron pattern by using one light and one dark weft. This is explained in chapter 2. The diagonal lines reverse direction when the wrist is rotated toward the body instead of away, making an S twist instead of a Z twist. Four rows of Z were followed by four rows of S. (Figure 5–3.)

When the twining was as long as the box, I slipped it off and turned it wrong side out. I then "twined off" the warp ends on the front. Directions for this will be found in chapter 12.

WRAPPING THE HANDLE

I wrapped the side warps in groups of four with the rug yarn. The wrapping causes groups to coil around one another. At intervals all of the groups were wrapped together for extra strength. (Figure 5–4.) After the wrapping had progressed some distance on each side, I tied each end from the left to a corresponding end from the right in a tight square knot. The knots were covered by the wrapping.

FINISHING THE FLAP

After a few rows entirely across the flap, warps were dropped in pairs on either side.

50

CHAPTER 6.

Twining As A Tapestry Technique

In ordinary weaving, weft threads cross the entire width of the fabric, from selvage to selvage, at right angles to the warp. Tapestry is a weaving technique in which the wefts are discontinuous. Instead of crossing the entire width, they go back and forth, each within its own color area. Traditionally, the weft is beaten down firmly so that none of the warp shows. In contemporary tapestry, however, the warp is sometimes allowed to be visible and contributes to the design.

If there are slits in the design, a weft will turn around the same warp a number of times, one row above the other, as it reaches the edge of a color area. This will also be true of the adjacent warp in the next color area, leaving a slit between the two areas of color. The result is called *slit tapestry*. (Figure 6–1.) In older times, the slits were sewn shut after the completion of the weaving, but in contemporary tapestry slits are often used as design motifs.

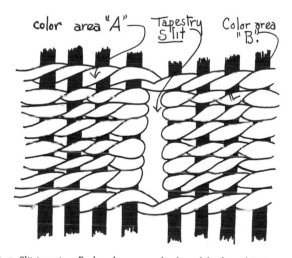

Figure 6–1. Slit tapestry. Each color moves back and forth within its own area.

Figure 6-2. A Chilkat blanket, front view.

Weft that does not follow the usual right-angled relation to the warp is called *eccentric*. I have great enthusiasm for eccentric weft, because it takes us farther away from machine-produced fabric than does the more usual horizontal weft.

I have been eager to see how the twining technique might lend itself to slit tapestry, especially tapestry with eccentric wefts. Most of the historic examples of great twining are geometric in design, and it was with the idea of being able to work more freely and with the hope of being able to take twining into new dimensions that I began to experiment.

Figure 6–3. A Chilkat blanket, back view.

I began by studying Chilkat blankets and noting how the design was often outlined by a twining which was also a braiding. Had the warps been pulled out of the completed work, a solid three-strand braid would have been left. This suggested the idea of incorporating braiding into twining. The braid I eventually used comes from the Philippines and is simpler than the Chilkat braid. Directions for an actual three-strand braid on warps are in chapter 4. The Chilkat blanket shown, both front and back views, illustrates clearly that each color moves back and forth in its own pattern area. (Figures 6–2 and 6–3.)

STARTING ECCENTRIC WEFTS

To begin an eccentric direction of weft, twine several rows of gradually decreasing length, as shown in the photograph. This paves the way for undulations in the rows that follow. (Figure 6–4.) The Philippine braid may be used whenever it is desirable to accent a curve. (Figure 6–5.)

In Jean Hudson's small red and pink tapestry, the design was invented as the work progressed. However, depending upon the work habits of the craftsman, work can also be planned in advance and a cartoon can be followed. The photograph of a small area shows the way in which rows of unequal length contribute to the eccentric direction of the wefts. (Figures 6–6 and 6–7.)

Figure 6–4. Decreasing rows of twining to prepare for eccentric wefts.

Figure 6–5. A row of Philippine Braid used to accentuate a curve formed by partial rows of twining.

Figure 6-7. Detail of tapestry in Figure 6-6, showing tapestry slit, eccentric weft, and use of braiding.

Figure 6-6. A twined tapestry in red and pink with eccentric weft and raised areas in Philippine braid by Jean Hudson.

Figure 6-8. Adding heavy warps for the Philippine Braid.

MAKING THE PHILIPPINE BRAID

The warps already present may be used for the braid or warps of a different size or color may be added. If you use the existing warps, the starting warp will be displaced, leaving a small gap. This is not usually of any consequence, as a second row of braiding in the opposite direction will return it to its original position.

If you add warps for the braiding, they may be inserted at midpoint of their length in adjacent twists of completed rows of twining. If the new warps are larger than those being used in the body of the work, insert in every other twist as opposed to every twist. (Figure 6–8.)

To braid from right to left, pick up the third warp to the left where the braiding is to start. Make a half hitch around the first two warps, as shown in the drawing. Pull it up snugly. Then let the end drop down into place parallel with the other warps. This is step one. (Figure 6–9.) Step two consists of picking up the fourth warp to the left and making a half hitch around the second two. Pull it up snugly and let the end fall down into place as in step one. (Figure 6–10.) Continue in this manner for the distance that is to be braided.

In braiding from left to right, the mirror image of the above takes place, as is shown in the drawings. (Figures 6–11 and 6–12.)

If the braiding is always done in the same direction, a diagonal edge is set up. (Figure 6–13.) The photograph also shows how to get rid of the added warps after an area of braiding has been completed. Twine each added warp tightly in place with a warp in the body of the work. After a couple of rows, drop it to the back, out of sight.

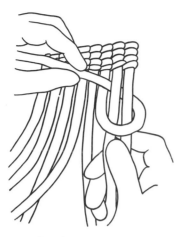

Figure 6-9. Braiding from right to left—step one.

Figure 6-11. Braiding from left to right—step one.

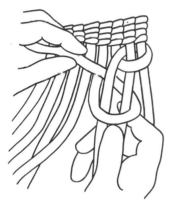

Figure 6-10. Braiding from right to left—step two.

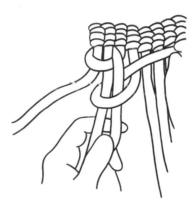

Figure 6-12. Braiding from left to right—step two.

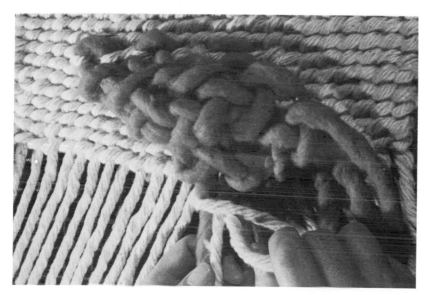

Figure 6-13. A diagonal edge is set up by beginning each row of braiding from the same side.

A TAPESTRY THAT GREW

The small red and pink tapestry, which was Jean Hudson's first experiment, encouraged a group of us to plan a much larger hanging. Jean dyed mop cord black for the warps, which she cut 6 feet long. Since she did not want to pull all of this length of warp through the twists, she started in the middle of the lengths by pinning a few warps to a piece of building board with T-pins. She did not know when she started how wide the tapestry might become, so at first she used only enough warps to twine the center of interest. The design came from a tissue paper collage she had previously completed. She did not attempt to follow the collage exactly, but only as a point of reference and departure. (Figures 6–14 and 6–15.)

Rug yarn in black, beige, browns, taupe, and related neutrals was used for weft, sometimes a number of strands at a time. As the number of weft strands used together varied in different parts of the work, a certain amount of rippling occurred. This seemed to add to the effect and was encouraged by changes of tension and by varying the number of yarns being used together.

The finished piece used up the entire length of the 6-foot warps. The warp ends were grouped and wrapped at the bottom. A wrapped dowel was used at the top for a hanger. (Figure 6–16.)

Figure 6–14. A tissue paper collage used as a guide for Jean Hudson's tapestry shown in Figure 6–16.

Figure 6–15. Beginning the tapestry in the center area.

58

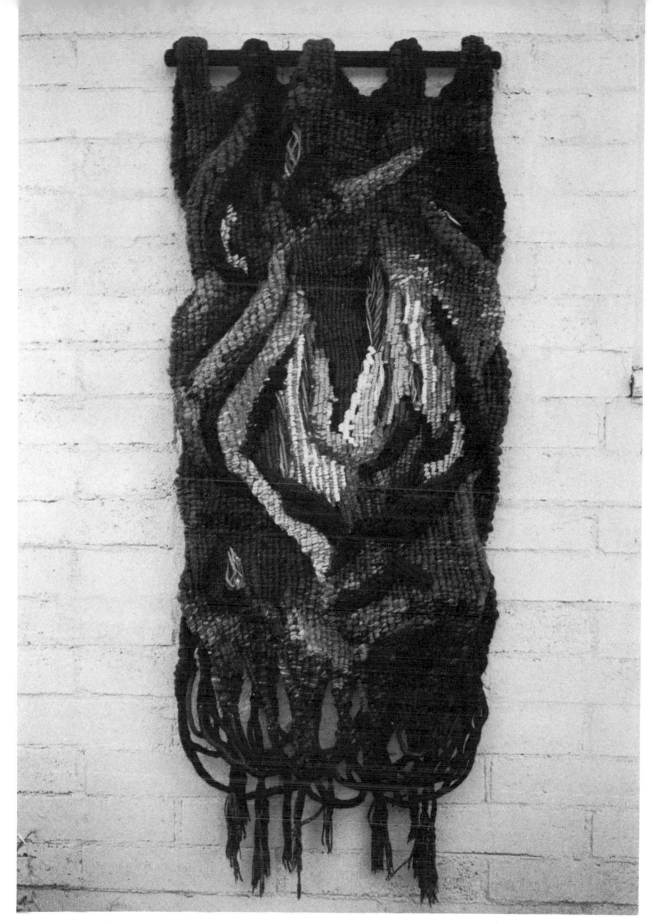

Figure 6-16 The finished tapestry by Jean Hudson in black, rust, grays, and taupe.

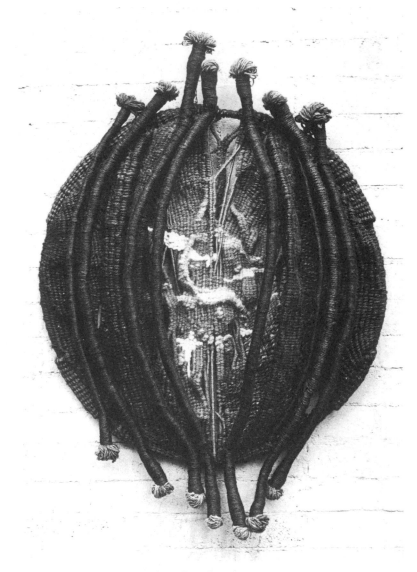

Figure 6–17. A tapestry twined in a hoop by Marjorie Trout.

A TWINED TAPESTRY IN A HOOP

Methods similar to Jean's were used by Marjorie Trout for twining a tapestry in an oak hoop. She began the twining in the center of the length of the warps, which were pinned to a piece of building board.

The work was inserted into the hoop after the center portion was completed and the wrapped bars across the front were added last. (Figure 6–17.)

ADDING WARPS TO MAKE A SECOND LAYER

Additional warps may be added in any area where the twining has been completed. The new warps are inserted at midpoint of their length by going behind any warp or weft yarn. In Dee Anderson's hanging some of the second layer of warps go behind warps and hang down vertically. The added warps at the center unit go behind weft units, which starts them out at right angles to the weaving that has been done. (Figures 6–18 and 6–19.)

THE ADVANTAGES OF TWINING A TAPESTRY

There are several advantages to twining a tapestry instead of weaving it in the ordinary way. One advantage is the lack of equipment. I am always looking for techniques that require a minimum of equipment. Except for a piece of building board and a few T-pins, these tapestries require none. The large materials used—thick jute and bundles of rug yarn—as well as the heavy mop cord, seem to be a liberating factor in working freely. While it is possible to use bulky fibers on a loom, most weavers tend to work with finer threads, which do not encourage freewheeling.

In a twined tapestry begun at the center area, the width can be increased at any time after the work is begun if the concept seems to call for a bigger statement. Also, you can shift the work about on a piece of building board so that it may be kept "right under your nose" while you sit in a chair in a comfortable position.

I look forward to seeing many fine twined tapestries as experimentation continues.

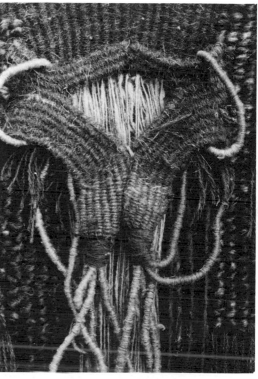

Figure 6-19. Detail of the tapestry shown in Figure 6-18, showing the use of added warps to form a center of interest.

Figure 6-18. A twined tapestry by Dee Anderson.

CHAPTER 7.

Dolls, Puppets, Critters, & Masks

Figure 7-1. A twined tubular shape is padded to make a doll by Barbara Kincaid.

Even small children are able to make delightful twinings. Simple shapes can be cut from cardboard and used as a guide for tension and for adding or dropping warps. A fantasy figure by Barbara Kincaid was twined over a rectangle of cardboard. The tubular shape was padded and sewn shut, top and bottom. (Figure 7-1.) A few variations on the basic rectangle produced other whimsical dolls of great character. The warps for the arms were attached to the twined body and twined around and around. (Figure 7-2.)

To twine birds Barbara cuts simplified bird shapes out of cardboard and ties a holding cord around the shape near the tip. Warps are added or dropped as needed to make the twining conform to the pattern and the wefts go around and around. Warps were tied onto the holding cord and twined to a point making the "head" end of the bird. (Figure 7-3.)

The doll shown in the photograph, twined by Candace Martin, started out to be a weed vase. The shape did not seem satisfactory to her and, in frustration, she turned it upside down and slammed it on the table. The thought then occurred to her that it might make a better doll than a vase, so she completed it as a doll with eyes and mouth suggested by a bit of black yarn. (Figure 7-4.)

The beady-eyed landlord with a horsehair beard was twined by Randall Hickcock as a hand puppet. He began the work at the top of the head and twined around and around as though it were a bag. (See chapter 1.) He dropped a few warps to make the neck and added a few for the shoulders. He added arms by attaching warps to the chest and back after they were twined. The chest and back were twined separately as flat pieces in order to leave a hole for the arms. Just below the arms, he again twined the work around and around as a cylinder. (Figure 7-5.)

Susan Gelfuso attached warps to the rim of a hoop to make a jute mask in countered twining. (Figure 7-6.)

Figure 7-3. Twining a bird form over a simplified cardboard shape by Barbara Kincaid.

Figure 7-2. A group of twined dolls by Barbara Kincaid.

Figure 7-6. Detail of a twined mask by Susan Gelfuso.

Figure 7-4. A twined doll by Candace Martin twined with jute and horsehair.

Figure 7-5. A twined puppet by Randall Hickok.

CHAPTER 8.

Taaniko: The Maori Method Of Twining

When Captain Cook rediscovered New Zealand in 1769, he found that the Maori people there had perfected a certain kind of twining to a high art form. The word *taaniko* is used to describe both the technique and the result. Flax was dyed red and black and used with natural white fiber to twine geometric patterns for headbands, cloak borders, kilt belts, and bodices. The taaniko bodice shown here is from the collection of Cay Garrett. (Figure 8–1.)

Maori girls learned the art from older women, copying traditional patterns. The isolation of the Maori people became less and less after Cook's visit and new influences brought changes in their art forms. Today the Maori continue to use old patterns, but often produce them with yarn on canvas instead of by taaniko twining. More about the art of taaniko may be learned from *The Art of Taaniko Weaving* by S.M. Mead, published by A.H. and A.W. Reed, Wellington.

You have already learned in chapter 2 that when twining with two wefts of different color, one rotation of the wrist in a half-twist brings each color to the top over alternate warps. You also learned that two rotations (it is obvious that two rotations means two half-twists, since the human wrist is incapable of making a full turn of 360 degrees) brings the *same* color continuously to the top surface. Thus, you may twine with one black and one white weft and produce a solid black (or solid white) top surface by making two half-twists between each warp. You saw in chapter 2 how the Indian women kept their chewed corn husk wefts on the outer surface of their bags by the use of two half-twists.

The Maori people also made use of this principle, but they introduced a third, and sometimes a fourth, weft. By pulling the tension more tightly on the back surface, these added strands are allowed to follow along passively until their color is needed on the surface to make the pattern. When three wefts are used, two run along behind the warps and one in front. To change the surface color a half-twist brings the new one to the top. As a guideline, any pattern which lends

Figure 8–1. A Taaniko bodice from New Zealand. From the collection of Cay Garrett.

Figure 8–2. A bag by B.J. Koch with patterned area done in taaniko twining.

Figure 8–3. A Coptic cross design by B.J. Koch.

itself to needlepoint may be twined by the taaniko method. When making an article with only a small area of taaniko twining, such as the bag by B.J. Koch shown, the three colors are carried not all around the bag, but only in the pattern area. (Figure 8–2.)

Graph paper is a convenient way to translate a design concept into a pattern. The inspiration for B.J. Koch's purple and gold twining was a Coptic cross from Lalibela, Ethiopia. The brass of the cross suggested the gold color yarn. The purple used for the background carries the feeling of ecclesiastical ritual and richness typical of the Coptic church. The churches of Lalibela are carved out of solid rock and have been in constant use since the twelfth century. Over the years many intricate variations of the cross motif have evolved. (Figure 8–3.)

An even older concept of the cross comes from western Africa and is preChristian. Lega, the chief loa (a god who descends to earth), is lord of the crossroads, and the cross is his symbol. Contrary to popular belief, the ceremonies of voodoo are not made to drive spirits away. Rather, they are performed to invoke spirits to descend to earth and possess people. Every sacred tree of the forest is, by virtue of its vertical position, a path from the sky by which the spirits of deceased ancestors come down to earth when properly invited. The damp earth, which is the origin of all life, is united with heaven by the roots and trunk of a sacred tree. The horizontal branches of a tree or the horizontal bar of a cross symbolizes the world, which we in the west think of as the "actual" or real world—people, creatures, plants. It is the all-important meeting place of the earthly and the divine—of the present moment in its intersection with eternity. Lega guards the spot.

Since the invisible ones are ancestors who once lived among men and after death dissolved into the dark waters below before they ascended to the spirit world above, the cross also stands for the unity of life and death. While contemplating this symbolism, Mel Kernahan made a simple doodlelike sketch in her notebook This was then transferred to graph paper and made symmetrical. The large finished twining followed the plotting of the design on the squared paper and is remarkably effective. (Figures 8–4, 8–5, and 8–6.)

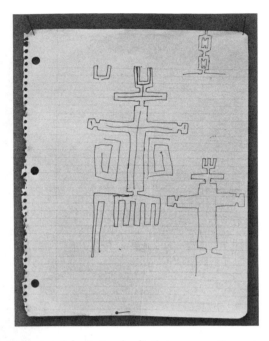

Figure 8–4. A beginning doodle that expresses the west African preChristian concept of the cross as a design.

Figure 8–5. Organizing the two-color design on graph paper.

Figure 8–6. The finished twining by Mel Kernahan.

Figure 8–7. Plotting a geometric design on graph paper. There are sixty-nine numbered squares in each direction. For easy reading paper with large squares should be used.

The precise and beautiful taaniko twining of the Maoris presented a challenge to Martha Bontems. She plotted a geometric design on graph paper, which was sixty-nine squares wide and sixty-nine squares long. She used paper with large squares for ease of reading. Black and red ink were used to indicate where those colors would appear in the twining. Rattail cord was the material used for both warp and weft. The finished work has the warp ends hanging to make a deep fringe. The twining will be used as the front of a bag. (Figures 8–7 and 8–8.)

The taaniko method of twining makes a sturdy fabric because of the extra wefts carried on the back surface. The examples shown are rectilinear in character, but there is no reason why curvilinear forms cannot be plotted on graph paper and reproduced in twining. The Maori method of handling passive warps on the back surface suggests a way to reinforce twined rugs by carrying along a passive weft, which need never surface for design reasons.

Figure 8–8. The finished purse front in black, red, and white rattail cord by Martha Bontems.

CHAPTER 9.

More Projects

A TWINED CRADLE

While waiting for her baby to be born, Fran Patten pondered about what kind of handmade cradle would be most suitable for an artist's child. A group of us strongly felt that to place a child in a plastic, machine-made container would be subjecting him too soon to the curses of our age. All of us applauded Fran for her desire to environ her child with something unique which was formed with imagination and love. (Figure 9–1.) If the cradle is set on the floor, it may be rocked on the two oak half-hoops which support it. When it is hung from a hook in the ceiling, it is a swing. When little Sean outgrows it, the cradle may be upended and hung as a swinging chair.

Sisal rope was used for the warps. The wefts are seine cord and cotton mop cord. A piece of electric conduit, bent in a racetrack shape, supports the upper edge beneath the twining, which is rolled over it. Mop cord is thick and soft and provides a pleasant textural contrast to the firmer, thinner seine cord. (Figure 9–2.)

Fran began the twining in the middle of the length of the warps. The cradle is about 4 feet long, but she cut the warps longer than that so that those which were not dropped in the shaping process could be wrapped and knotted at the ends. The shaping, which she accomplished by grouping warps two as one and then dropping one, is very much like that of the boat-shaped basket from Ethiopia shown in Figure. (Figure 9–3.) She drilled holes in the oak rockers near the top edge so they could be very sturdily attached to the twining and used seine cord to lash the rockers to the twining in a decorative way. (Figure 9–4.) Some of the warp ends of sisal were hidden under the rolled rim, but others were wrapped and tied in a decorative knot. (Figure 9–5.) When the twining was completed, Fran cut a piece of building board, or cellotex, with a sharp knife and covered it with muslin to make a firm bottom. This bottom is removable. The sides are also pieces of building board covered with muslin in rainbow colors. When the cradle hangs from the ceiling, it is suspended by sturdy sisal ropes, which attach to hooks in the beams. Should the cradle need cleaning, it can be scrubbed with a small brush and a concentrated detergent, and then rinsed by hosing it down.

Figure 9–1. A twined cradle by Fran Patten.

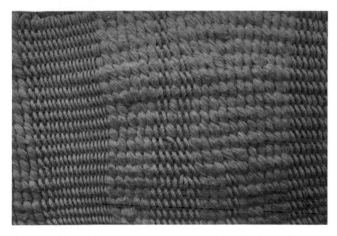

Figure 9–2. Textural contrast between mop cord and seine cord.

Figure 9–4. Holes were drilled near the ends of the oak rockers and rockers were lashed to cradle with decorative wrapping.

Figure 9–3. Bottom view of the cradle, showing basketlike shaping. Oak half-circles support the cradle when it is hung and act as rockers when it is sitting.

Figure 9–5. End view of cradle, showing the finishing knot.

Figure 9–6. Millard, the Dendel rabbit, stretches out on a wool twined rug.

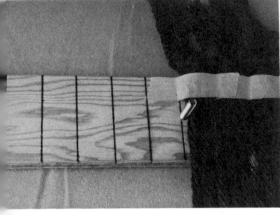

Figure 9–7. Masking tape holds the warps in place while they are arranged, three to the inch, on the bottom board of a clamp.

Figure 9–8. When all the warps are in place, the top board of the clamp is set in place and held tight with wing nuts.

A TWINED RUG

There is just nothing like stretching out full length on the all-wool pile of a twined rug. Millard, the Dendel rabbit, knows this is true and so do we. (Figure 9–6.)

Large cotton mop cord was dyed a dark green for Jo Dendel's rug, which measures 46 by 84 inches. The weft and pile are heavy, all-wool rug yarn. A little experimenting showed that three warps per inch would place them snugly together. Jo made a clamp to hold the warps, which consisted of two strips of plywood bolted together. Inch spaces were marked off on the top of the lower board to assist in spacing the warps. The warps were tied in pairs with an overhand knot just above the edge of the clamp. These knots kept the warp from pulling through the clamp. Masking tape held the warps in place while they were being arranged. (Figure 9–7.)

When all the warps were in place, the upper board of the clamp was placed over the lower board. The two were held together by fastening wing nuts over the bolts, which are spaced at 6-inch intervals. (Figure 9–8.) The clamp could then be hung in any convenient place. Jo hung it from a frame and stretched white cords on the frame as a guideline for the selvage. (Figure 9–9.)

Figure 9-9. The clamp with warps in place is hung on a frame. White strings made a selvage guide.

Figure 9-11. The back side of the rug shown in Figure 9-6. The rows of light color seen are the backs of the Ghiordes knots.

Figure 9-10. The Ghiordes knot.

A pile surface was made by making one row of Ghiordes knots after every five rows of twining. The yarn for the Ghiordes knots was cut in 4-inch lengths on a paper cutter. To make the knot, two warps are encircled and the ends of the knotting yarn are brought up between them, as shown in the drawing. (Figure 9-10.) The Ghiordes knot is named after a town in Turkey where rugs have been knotted for many generations. It is sometimes called the Turkish knot.

The colors in the rug are golds, oranges, and greenish yellows. These show up on the back of the rug as light stripes against the moss green color of the twining. (Figure 9-11.) The fringe at the ends of the rug was formed by wrapping each warp with green rug yarn and making an overhand knot at the very end of each warp.

Figure 9–13. The twining in Figure 9–12 worn as a special occasion costume.

Figure 9–14. The back view of the wrapped-rope twining.

Figure 9–12. "Night Flight," a wrapped-rope twining by Roméo Reyña—seen against the sky.

A PROJECT IN WRAPPED ROPE

The craft project shown here is heavy and huge and incredibly beautiful. Slim and elegant gold cords encircle ropes as thick as my thumb. The ropes have been wrapped in blue and bluish gray yarn. Some of them are spaced slightly apart by blue beads of Egyptian paste. Viewers wish to see the blue and the gold stretched out and against a background of sky. (Figure 9–12.) There is a hole in the center of the length which immediately suggests an opening for the head. Trying it on calls for assistance, however. I guess the weight at about 75 pounds. No ordinary garment, this. Once it settles over the body, the weight of the back counterbalances the weight of the front, so wearing it for some very special occasion or presentation would be entirely possible.

Wearing it is exactly what entertainer Almeta Speaks did for an important opening night. The winglike shoulders support their own weight. In the photograph, Almeta's arms are at her side, even though one can easily imagine that they are extended outward for flight. (Figure 9–13.) The back view shows the "train" formed by the trailing ends of rope cascading to the floor. (Figure 9–14.)

(continued on page 77)

1

2

3

4

1. This twined cradle made of sisal, seine cord, and mop cord may be hung from ceiling or rocked on oak half-hoops. Created by Fran Patten for her son.

2. A warp-twined bag was made by twining two rectangles, one larger than the other to allow for the flap, and then sewing them together. Created by Jonda Friel.

3. The design of this basket is simple and sturdy. Jute was used for the warps and the twining was done with raffia. Created by Cindy Wallace.

4. In this tapestry warps were added to create a second layer and an interesting effect. Created by Dee Anderson.

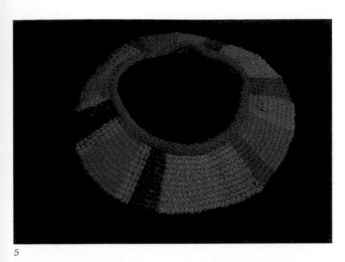

5

7

8

9

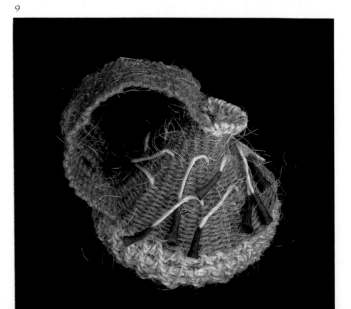

6

10

11

12

5. A circular collar shaped by adding partial rows of wefts. Notice the "Ballerino Roll" on the inside edge. Created by Louella Ballerino.

6. This pile rug was made with wool and cotton mop cord. The pile was achieved by making a row of Ghiordes knots after every five rows of twining. Created by Jo Dendel.

7. The idea for this twined wall hanging came from a Japanese rain cape. The soft fibers used allow it to flow gently as a garment. Created by Rosita Montgomery.

8. Part of a magnificent twined ceiling in the Seven Olives Hotel in Lalibela, Ethiopia. Photograph courtesy of Cindy Hickok.

9. Eucalyptus seeds adorn this sisal basket; yet they do not detract from its beautiful shape. Created by Helen Hennessey.

10. "Night Flight." A beautifully styled wrapped-rope twining is worn here as an opening night costume by this singer. Created by Roméo Reyña.

11. The back view of "Night Flight," showing the train cascading to the floor. The materials used were gold cord and thick rope.

12. A richly striped pillow front done in countered twining. Created by Louella Ballerino.

13. Done in the taaniko method of twining, the idea for this cross came from a Coptic cross seen by the artist in Lalibela, Ethiopia. Created by B.J. Koch.

14. A twined bag of glowing oranges and rich earth tones. Created by Helen Hennessey.

15. An enjoyable project to work on is this twined doll-puppet. Created by Jill Hickok.

16. Techniques of warp twining and weft twining were combined to make this truly magnificent cape. Rug yarn and chenille were used and buckeyes and eucalyptus pods adorn the cape.

13

15

14

16

Figure 9–15. Detail showing the tension control in "Night Flight."

Figure 9–16. "Night Flight" as a wall hanging.

The beginning, as well as the end, of each row of gold weft has wrapped ends, making a fringe along both sides. The tension of the top weft was kept tighter than that of the lower weft, which gives the top weft the appearance of having been couched down. (Figure 9–15.)

When Roméo Reyña started this impressive project, he first wrapped yards and yards of rope, which went on and on seemingly without beginning or end. When the entire length of rope had been wrapped, Roméo started to make it into a composition by feeding it out over the grass of his lawn. Starting with one end, which was arranged in an oval, Roméo walked around and around the beginning oval until eight consecutive rows had been formed. Following the pattern of these first eight rows along the sides of the oval, Roméo than stretched out the rope which forms the sides. With a bit of rearranging of spacing the designing was done. There remained to be done only the twining at intervals across the areas of rope, which were needed to hold the areas where they had been placed.

Roméo's work is pure play, pure invention. "Night Flight" probably will hang on a wall with a high ceiling more than it will be worn as a garment. (Figure 9–16.) Either way, it speaks to us of celebration, of fantasy, and of old rituals where gold caught the light and enriched an occasion. This is a craft object with "presence."

(continued from page 72)

CHAPTER 10.

Twining As Sculpture

Twining is an ideal technique for fiber sculpture. Sturdy warps provide a very firm structure which naturally lends itself to modeling and to making pieces with a third dimension.

An off-white sculptural twining by Jeannie Freeland charms with its simplicity. The sisal warps are hung from a bleached bone. The vertebra bone, lower down, serves a function. It is not extraneous and does not appear to be "stuck on" without purpose because it is used to hold strips in place. The weft is bleached sisal and the fringe is unspun sisal, sometimes called "box sisal." (Figures 10–1 and 10–2.)

A weaverbird nest from western Africa provided Josephine Granger with the inspiration for a nestlike hanging. A weaverbird nest is a sculptural marvel. With some mysterious knowledge the weaverbirds turn the entrance to their nest away from the branch so that snakes cannot reach their eggs or their young. The entrance hole is made in the side of the nest rather than the bottom, which prevents the young from falling out. (Figures 10–3 and 10–4.)

It is quite impossible to give directions for a twined sculpture, and it would not be desirable to do so even if it were possible because these should be one-of-a-kind statements and should not be reproduced. It is even difficult for the artist to prethink the work. One stage seems to lead into another. However, a few general suggestions are helpful.

To begin a three-dimensional shape, it is sometimes helpful to twine over a beach ball or other spherical form. If numerous slits are left, these are available for the insertion of strips of twining later. (Figure 10–5.) Usually, it is easier to start in the center area of a work and allow it to grow toward either end. In the large sisal twining by Ann Dreyer, a hollow tree was the inspiration. (Figure 10–6.) The frail shell of the ancient growth supported a tangle of vines. Wrapped warp ends suggest roots. (Figure 10–7.) New warps were added whenever longer strands or more additional strands were needed.

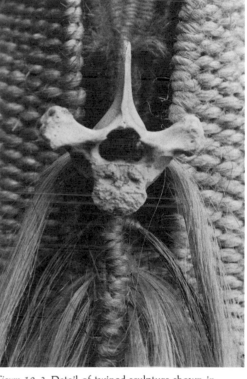

Figure 10-2. Detail of twined sculpture shown in Figure 10-1 showing tied-in box sisal.

Figure 10-1. An off-white twined sculpture by Jeannie Freeland.

Figure 10–4. A sculptured nest inspired by the weaverbird nest by Josephine Granger.

Figure 10–3. A weaverbird nest from western Africa.

Figure 10–5. Twining over a beach ball.

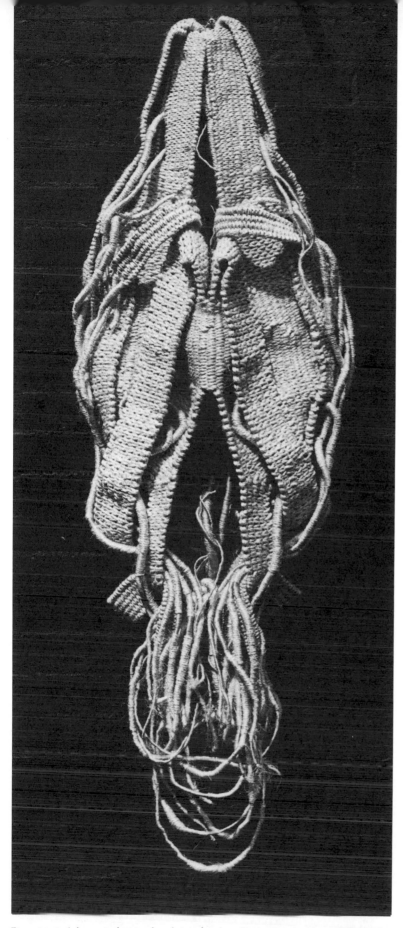

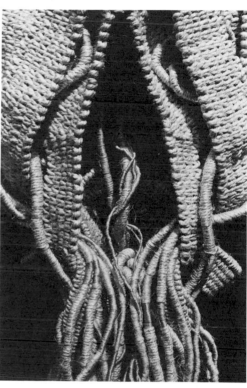

Figure 10-7. Detail of the twined sculpture shown in Figure 10-6.

Figure 10-6. A large sisal twined sculpture by Ann Dreyer inspired by a hollow tree.

Figure 10-8. A sisal wall hanging by Nancy Lacy.

Figure 10-9. A sisal wall piece by Ann Dreyer.

Figure 10-10. "Ear of Corn" by Doris Fox.

Jute and sisal are both excellent materials for making sculptural wall pieces because they are firm enough to give rigidity to the work. Sisal rope in natural creamy white was used for warps by Nancy Lacy. (Figure 10-8.) Her hanging, which is 3⅓ by 3 feet with a depth of 6 inches, is really a modified shallow basket. The warp ends are untwisted to make a dense fringe all around the piece. Goat's hair and raffia in gray and black were used for the twining.

The sculptural quality of Ann Dreyer's hanging (Figure 10-9) was achieved by turning the strips, allowing the underside to come to the top. This hanging is 7 by 5½ feet. It was designed by manipulating strips of cut paper.

An ear of corn was the inspiration for Doris Fox's three-dimensional twining. The warps are heavy jute. Twining was done with raffia which has been dyed red. Unspun sisal, dyed a rusty orange, represents the corn silk. The husks are made of bleached jute.

Twining began in the middle of the length of the warps and proceeded around and around. The warps were dropped to the inside to taper the shape. When one half was finished it was padded with Dacron®. The other half was padded as the twining progressed. (Figure 10-10.)

CHAPTER 11.

Twining On Fixed Warps

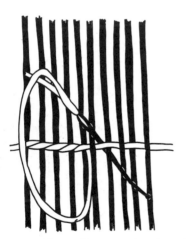

Figure 11-1. Making a Z twist, working from left to right on fixed warps.

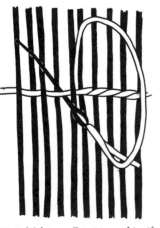

Figure 11-2. Making a Z twist, working from right to left on fixed warps.

Some craftsmen, especially loom weavers who are accustomed to working with taut warps, prefer to twine on fixed warps, rather than having one set of ends loose. There are several simple devices for securing warp under tension. Metal or wooden hoops may be warped or the warp may be wrapped around an empty picture frame, a piece of Masonite® may be notched at regular intervals to receive the warp or nails may be driven into a frame and the warp carried around each nail.

With fixed warps the weft may be wound into small bobbins or threaded through needles. In my own work, I use large curved needles which have ball points and big eyes. Each weft end is threaded through a needle. The wefts are led into position with the needles instead of using twists of the wrist.

There is a method of twining very rapidly which involves going over and under alternate warps with one weft for an entire row, while letting the other threaded weft do the actual twining. The slant of the needle on the return row is important. To make a Z twist when working from left to right, pass the needle under each warp that has a weft over it, with the needle pointing toward the body. (Figure 11-1.) If the needle doing the twining is working from right to left, pass the needle under each warp that has a weft over it. The slant of the needle should be away from the body. (Figure 11-2.) To make an S twist, the direction of the slant of the needle is the reverse.

In needle twining, it is important not to pull the first or "running stitch row" too tightly, as the work is more attractive when the tension is the same in both wefts. Needle twining can be introduced into any regular weaving when there is an area where it is particularly desirable to completely cover the warps. It is also a good device to establish the spacing of warps. The striped bag, twined on fixed warp by Irma Switzer, was made as a long runner which was folded in half. This gives vertical stripes, since the warps run from side to side. An Egyptian braid covers the seam at the sides where the bag was sewn together. (Figure 11-3.)

Figure 11-3. A bag made by twining on fixed warps by Irma Switzer.

Figure 11–4. A fixed warp twining in a metal hoop by the author entitled "Partial Eclipse."

Figure 11–5. Detail of the fixed warp twining shown in Figure 11–4.

If a hoop is to be warped, it is sometimes desirable to make half hitches or buttonhole stitches in which to anchor the warps around the edge. This was the method I used to warp my "Partial Eclipse." The warp yarn is a thick and thin handspun, which is not completely covered by the wefts. (Figure 11–4.) A second layer of twining partially eclipses the back layer. This layer was twined with loose ends. Twining in the center area of heavy yarns, I began tapering the shape by dropping warps to the back. These were allowed to hang down vertically and form a fringe. When only two warps remained over which to twine, I tied them in a monkey fist knot and attached them to the edge of the work. I spread the untwined section of warp out in a fan shape and attached it to the left edge of the hoop. (Figure 11–5.)

Figure 11-6. A large hoop done in fixed warp twining by the author.

When I twined a large 3⅔-foot wooden hoop, I turned the project into an experiment for a new way of warping. Very often large hoops are difficult to work with because they change shape under the tension of the warp. I first twined the padded section in the middle of the hanging. This was done on a separate round piece of notched Masonite®. I made two twined circles, sewed them together at the edges, and padded the shape just as though it was to be a pillow. I then cut numerous warps, twice as long as the distance from the rim of the hoop to the padded area, plus a few inches for tying. I wrapped these strands at midpoint of their length and bent the wrapped part around the rim of the hoop. I then brought the loose ends to the edge of the padded circle and tied them to form the fringe around it. (Figure 11-6.)

The warps which were tied into the circle were sufficiently long for twining to begin. Additional warps were needed soon and were added in the manner described in chapter 3. The photograph shows the appearance of the twining in areas where only a few warps have been added and in other areas where many warps have been added. A few rows of twining near the outer edges stabilized the position of the newly arrived warps. (Figure 11-7.) The fringe around the outside edge of the hoop is made from the tied ends of added warps. The smoothness with which the added warps fit into the work is shown in the detail. (Figure 11-8.)

Figure 11-7. The hoop shown in Figure 11-6 in process, showing areas where warp has been added after the start of the weaving.

Figure 11-8. Detail of the twining in Figure 11-6, showing added warps worked in smoothly.

CHAPTER 12.

Alternate Methods Of Securing Warps

The pillow in chapter 1 was begun by tying the warps in place with lark's head knots. I will now describe two alternate methods of beginning a twining.

HANGING THE WARPS FROM A BRAID

The advantage of this method over the use of lark's head knots is that the braid from which the warps are hung spaces the warps evenly. In cylindrical work the braid encircles the building board over which you are working. In flat work the braid is pinned to the top surface of the board. Some of the yarns are cut longer than are needed for the braiding and become warp ends, eliminating the necessity for a knot. For a circular project there are six steps.

Step one: To encircle a 12-inch board, cut one cord 5 feet long. Fifteen inches from one end, secure it to the building board with a T-pin. This is the warp with ends A and D in the drawing. Cut a second cord somewhat longer, say 7½ feet. (These measurements will vary a little with the thickness of the material being used.) Middle this cord, and, at the midpoint of its length, encircle the first cord with it where the pin enters the board. Pin it in place. I will call the ends of this cord B and C. (Figure 12–1.)

Step two: Bend the top of the first cord—end A—until it lies beside the two ends—B and C. The lone end D, which hangs down from the pin, is the first warp. (Figure 12–2.) Making an ordinary pigtail braid with the three ends—A, B, and C—encircle the board with ordinary pigtail braiding.

Step three: When the board is encircled with the braid, allow two of the three ends to hang down as warps. Bring the third end through the second lower loop from the opposite end to join the braid. End D is occupying the first loop. (Figure 12–3.) You now have the working board encircled with a braid from which four warps are hanging.

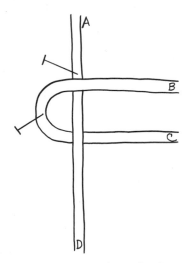

Figure 12-1. Hanging warps from a braid—step one.

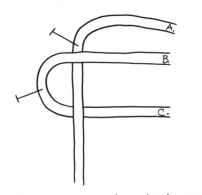

Figure 12-2. Hanging warps from a braid—step two.

Figure 12–3. Hanging warps from a braid—step three.

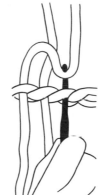

Figure 12–5. Hanging warps from a braid—step five.

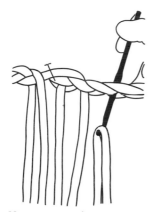

Figure 12–4. Hanging warps from a braid—step four.

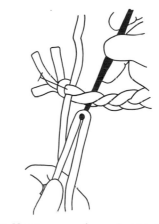

Figure 12–6. Hanging warps from a braid—step six.

Step four: The additional warps to be added are cut 2½ feet long (after middling, each one will hang 1¼ feet below the braided edge). Insert a crochet hook, pointing downward, in the lower strand of the first empty loop in the braid and pull a warp at midpoint of its length up through this loop. Half the length will now be above the braid (1¼ feet) and half below it (1¼ feet). (Figure 12–4.)

Step five: In the next loop to the right, pull another warp through the braid. (Figure 12–5.)

Step six: Two warps now extend above the braid. Hook the first one to have been brought upward with the crochet hook and bring it *down* through the first empty loop to the right. (Figure 12–6.) Continue in this manner until a warp end hangs down from each lower strand of braiding. If you desire double warps, which is a possibility if the warp material is light in weight, simply pull a second yarn at midpoint through each loop of braid.

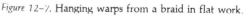

Figure 12–7. Hanging warps from a braid in flat work.

Hanging the warps from a pigtail braid in this manner spaces them out evenly and is a highly recommended way to begin, especially for cylindrical objects like the pillow in chapter 1. In a flat piece of work the process is similar except that there is no circle to close. End D simply becomes the first warp and the last three warps are the ends of the braided strands; or the braid may be finished at each end with an overhand knot. (Figure 12–7.)

Figure 12–8. Twining warps in place—step one.

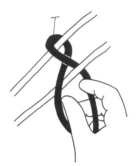

Figure 12–9. Twining warps in place—step two.

Figure 12–10. Twining warps in place—step three.

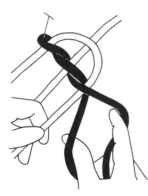

Figure 12–11. Twining warps in place—step four.

TWINING THE WARPS IN PLACE

This method of securing warps actually twines them in place. It is a little more involved than hanging warps from a braid, but it is not difficult to do if the directions are read with working material in hand and are followed step by step. As in the other two methods which have been described, the warps are cut twice the length of the project plus a few inches for grasping and finishing. One weft, or twining yarn, is needed in addition to the warps. Cut it about 2 yards long. With the warps cut and placed parallel and close at hand you are ready to begin.

Step one: Find the middle of the weft yarn and the middle of the length of the first *warp*. Wrap the warp with the middled weft and twist. (Figure 12–8.)

Step two: Find the middle point of the second warp. Place it next to the twist in the wefts which was made in step 1. (Figure 12–9.)

Step three: Give the wefts another half-twist, taking the one which rests over the warp to the bottom and the one which is under the warp to the top. There are now two warp ends projecting toward you. (Figure 12–10.)

Step four: Bring the first warp end from above the work down toward you. Bring it between the wefts and allow it to lie parallel to the first two warps ends below the twining. Again, give a half-twist to the wefts. (Figure 12–11.)

Step five: Add another warp—the third length of warp yarn—at midpoint of its length and again, give a half-twist to the wefts. Two warp ends now project away from you above the line of twining and four ends are below it. (Figure 12–12.)

Step six: Grasp the far end of the second warp which was added and bring it down between the wefts. Five ends are now pointing toward you below the line of twining and one warp is above it. (Figure 12–13.)

Step seven: Twist the wefts as usual. Continue until all the warps have been added. (Figure 12–14.)

Step eight: At the conclusion, one warp end lies above the line of twining. Bring it down and twist the wefts. (Figure 12–15.)

Step nine: Join the warps in a complete circle by twining the weft over the first warp, thus beginning the second row. (Figure 12–16.)

If the work is flat, instead of cylindrical, simply pull the last warp which is above the work down and parallel to the other warps and turn back.

Figure 12–12. Twining warps in place—step five.

Figure 12–13. Twining warps in place—step six.

Figure 12–14. Twining warps in place—step seven.

Figure 12–15. Twining warps in place—step eight.

Figure 12–16. Twining warps in place—step nine.

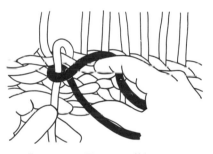

Figure 12–17. Twining off—step one.

FINISHING THE ENDS BY TWINING OFF

This method of finishing off actually twines the warps in place on the back, or wrong side, of the work. Turn the work so the back side faces upward and the warps to be disposed of point away from you. Middle a length of weft yarn and follow the simple steps shown in the drawings.

Step one: Bend the second warp from the left edge toward you, down over the body of the work, and enclose it with the middled weft. Pin the weft in place and make a half-twist. (Figure 12–17.) If the work being finished is cylindrical, you may bend down any one of the warp ends, counting that one as the "second" warp in the series.

Step two: Bring the first warp at the left edge behind the third warp from the left edge and down toward you between the wefts. Twist the wefts. (Figure 12–18.)

Step three: Take the third warp end behind the fourth and down through the wefts.

Continue in this way until all the warp ends have been twined off. You may twine a second row of weft across the warps for extra security. The ends may be snipped off evenly a short distance below the twined rows. (Figure 12–19.)

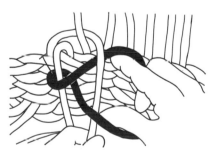

Figure 12–18. Twining off—step two

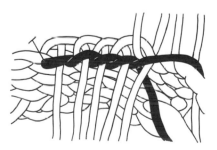

Figure 12–19. Twining off—step three.

91

CHAPTER 13.

Warp Twining

Once you've mastered weft twining you might want to try your hand at warp twining.

Warp twining has sometimes been called "Hungarian Weaving." However, it is done in many places in the world in addition to Hungary, so it seems more accurate to name it for the process rather than for the place.

In warp twining the warps are twisted instead of the weft. When determining warp lengths some allowance must be made for "take-up." As a rule of thumb, count on one-third of the length being used by the twist. As always, some additional length is needed for grasping the ends—usually 3 or 4 inches. The determined length is then doubled because each warp will be middled and hung on a holding cord. For instance, if a pillow is to be 1¼ feet deep when completed, figure 15 inches plus one-third of 15, or 5 inches, for take-up, plus 4 inches for grasping the ends. This adds up ·to twenty-four inches. Doubling this gives you a length of 48 inches or 4 feet. The number of warps needed depends on the diameter of the yarn and the size of the project. Make a little test sample to determine the number of warps per inch.

Two flat pieces were twined and sewn together at the edges to make Jonda Friel's bag. She made one rectangle longer than the other to form a flap. (Figure 13–1.) In making the purse it was not necessary to add any warps as the work progressed. But in other projects, the crown of a hat, for instance, warps are added as the size increases. You will first learn to twine a plain rectangle. Then you will learn how to move color about and then how to add in extra warps. To twine a cylinder, cut a piece of building board the desired width and twine around and around it, instead of going back and forth as one does in a flat piece of work. The following directions are for plain warp twining. I have divided these into seven easy steps. The warps have been measured as described above and hung on a holding cord. It is important that the total number of warps be divisible by four.

Figure 13–1. A warp-twined bag by Jonda Friel.

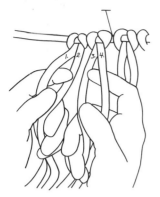

Figure 13-2. Warp twining—step one.

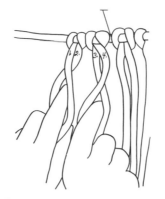

Figure 13-3. Warp twining—step two.

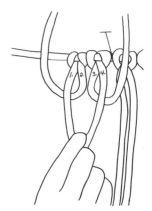

Figure 13-4. Warp twining—step three.

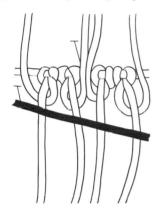

Figure 13-5. Warp twining—step four.

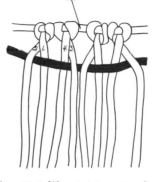

Figure 13-6. Warp twining—step five.

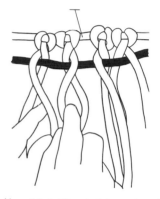

Figure 13-7. Warp twining—step six.

SEVEN STEPS IN WARP TWINING

Step one: Pick up the first group of four warps at the left edge of the work. If these four are numbered from left to right—1, 2, 3, 4—lift 1 and 4 with the index fingers in a motion preparatory to placing these warps between 2 and 3. (Figure 13-2.)

Step two: Bring the outside warp 1 over 2 and warp 4 over 3. They lie parallel in the lower shed. (A shed is the space between an upper and a lower plane of warps which have been temporarily separated to allow for the passage of the weaving thread.) (Figure 13-3.)

Step three: Lift warps 2 and 3 into the upper shed and let them rest above the line of mounting braid. (Figure 13-4.)

Step four: When a shed has been made across all of the warps, pin a length of weft yarn temporarily at the left side of the work and carry it across to the right side. In the case of cylindrical work, work on one side of the board at a time. After a few rows, the pin may be removed. Thread the weft end in a needle and work it to the wrong side. (Figure 13-5.)

Step five: Bring the upper shed (the warps above the work) down over the weft. (Figure 13-6.)

Step six: The beginning manipulation is now repeated. The outside members of each group of four are brought in and down and the remaining two are raised as in steps 2 and 3. (Figure 13-7.)

Step seven: The weft is returned through the new shed and the work continues in this manner. After raising the upper shed, tug on both sheds at the same time to pack the weft in place. (Figure 13-8.)

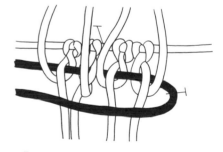

Figure 13-8. Warp twining—step seven.

Figure 13-9. A warp-twined necklace by Jonda Friel in which colors move diagonally.

MOVING COLORS DIAGONALLY

As Jonda Friel experimented with warp twining, it occurred to her that the colors could travel diagonally across the work and that the pattern need not be confined to parallel stripes. This idea opened up almost unlimited design possibilities. In her necklace the darks move not only out from the center, but back toward it again. The weft yarn has been pulled out at the selvage to form decorative "ears." The colors are purple and gold. Some of the yarns are chenille, which gives richness and variety to the work. (Figure 13-9.)

Step one: Set up the warps with eight dark warps in the center of a unit. This allows a unit of four to move in each direction. Weave two or more rows in order to space and stabilize the work. To begin we will be working with the warps left of the center. Change the sheds, but do not raise them above the work. (Figure 13-10.)

Step two: Make a "sandwich" by bringing the upper shed of the dark warps over the four adjacent light ones. The inside dark warps go under the four light ones. You can think of the light warps as the filling in this "sandwich." The lights and darks exchange places. (Figure 13-11.)

Step three: Working with the eight warps at the right of center, make a "sandwich" in the way described in step 2. (Figure 13-12.)

Step four: Change sheds in the usual way and bring the weft through the shed. (Figure 13-13.)

You are now ready to repeat the process if you wish to continue the diagonal movement. If you wish to bring the warps down parallel, continue as in plain warp twining. Give a little extra tug to the sheds to pack the weft firmly and to avoid a small hole where the colors exchange places. With the lower shed in the left hand and the upper shed in the right hand, it is easy to compact the wefts by pulling the two sets of warps in opposite directions.

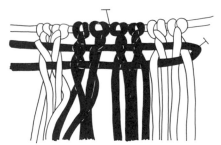

Figure 13-10. Moving colors—step one.

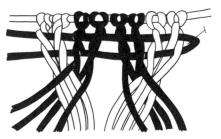

Figure 13-12. Moving colors—step three.

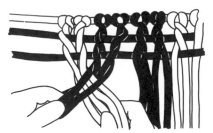

Figure 13-11. Moving colors—step two.

Figure 13-13. Moving colors—step four.

The dark warps can be moved back to the original position whenever you wish. The small sampler shows this happening on the fifth row after the first exchange of color. (Figure 13-14.)

Rug yarn, handspun wool, and chenille are the materials I used in the bag shown here. The handle was twined as a separate strip and attached at the base of the cylindrical twining. The bag is lined in red to match the chenille and has a zipper closing. Yarns from the front are tied to corresponding yarns in the back to make the bottom closing. Two front yarns and two back yarns are grouped together. Then, one of the four is tied in a tight overhand knot around the other three. (Figure 13-15.)

The other bag shown is by Mary Young and was begun at the bottom instead of the top. The top is finished with two rows of countered weft twining. The handle is an integral part, having been twined as part of the bag from the beginning. Extra length in the warps was necessary for the strips that make the handle. (Figure 13-16.) This bag was begun by using only a few warps attached to a ring of yarn. Additional warps were added as needed, as the bottom widened.

Figure 13-14. A sampler showing return of warps to original position.

Figure 13-15. A bag in warp twining by the author done in rug yarn, wool, and chenille.

Figure 13-16. A warp-twined bag begun at the center bottom by Mary Young.

95

ADDING WARPS

It is necessary to add warps in groups of four. Cut two warps the proper length and simply lay them in place at midpoint of the length over the weft of the previous row. This is step one. (Figure 13–17.) Step two consists of making a shed with the new warps just as though they had been there all along. (Figure 13–18.) If eight warps are to be added instead of four, twine one row with four new ones and add the second four on the next row.

The crown of a hat, which was twined by Rae Kipf, shows how you can begin with a small ring of yarn and add warps as needed. The band and brim section are weft twined and laid over a black straw brim. (Figure 13–19.) The lampshade, which Bici Linklater twined, has warps added in the same manner. Both the lampshade and the hat crown were twined with threads pulled from drapery remants. (Figure 13–20.)

Figure 13-17. Adding warps—step one.

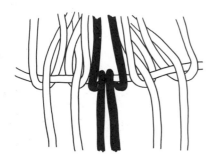

Figure 13-18. Adding warps—step two.

Figure 13-19. A warp-twined hat by Rae Kipf.

Figure 13–20. A warp-twined lampshade by Bici Linklater.

VARYING THE COMPACTNESS
OF THE TWINING

Warp twining may completely cover the wefts or it may be spaced so that the wefts show. Bula Rollyson used treated and untreated (dark and light) jute to make a plant stand. She worked over a sturdy hatbox. The darker jute was used for weft and it appears like a lattice on which the warp twining seems to be "climbing" with a life of its own, akin to a plant. (Figure 13–21.) This twining began at the center of the top. Middled warps were added, as needed, by hanging them over the previous row of weft until the rim of the box was reached.

Figure 13–21. A warp-twined plant stand by Bula Rollyson.

Figure 13-23. Beginning the cape. Warps were hung on a four-strand round braid.

Figure 13-24. Detail of a design motif of the cape.

Figure 13-25. Detail showing bottom finish of cape.

Figure 13-22. Weft twining and warp twining were combined in this cape by Joana Gosley.

A TWINED CAPE

Weft twining was combined with warp twining in a spectacular cape by Joana Gosley. (Figure 13-22.) Rug yarn, thick and thin handspun, and chenille in greens and gold were the materials used. The work was begun by making a holding cord of four-strand, round braid to encircle the neck. The beginning warps were hung on this braid. (Figure 13-23.) Additional warps were soon needed to follow the pattern for the cape. This pattern was cut from pellon and pinned to a dressmaker's board with T-pins. The warps were added as described in this chapter.

The shoulders and top part of the cape were quite solidly twined. In the lower section, in order to avoid excessive weight, Joana started to use weft twining spaced out at intervals of about 1 inch. However, the pattern area of the stripes continued as warp twining. When a row of weft reached the stripe, it simply hooked into the edge of the strip where it was tied with a square knot.

Buckeyes were used in the center of some of the oval design units. (Figure 13-24.) The bottom of the cape was finished with four-strand round braids, each of which terminates in a drilled eucalyptus pod. (Figure 13-25.)

Suppliers

The suppliers listed here will be able to provide you with the materials you'll need for twining.

Denwar Craft Studio
236 East 16th Street
Costa Mesa, California 92627

Greentree Ranch Wools
220 Linden Street
Fort Collins, Colorado 80521

Ironstone Warehouse
P.O. Box 196
2 South Main
Uxbridge, Massachusetts 01569

Las Manos, Inc.
12215 Coit Road
Dallas, Texas 75251

Some Place
2990 Adeline Street
Berkeley, California 94703

Straw Into Gold
P.O. Box 2904
5533 College Avenue
Oakland, California 94618

Index

Page numbers in italics indicate illustrations.